Love Starts Here

Finding Love Within For a Life Never Without

Love Starts Here

Finding Love Within For a Life Never Without

Nala Asa Shakur

Tyler Alese Norman

The All Natural

The All Natural
TheAllNatural, LLC

2nd Addition

ISBN: 979-8-218-95264-8 (Hardback)
ISBN: 979-8-218-95265-5 (Ebook)

Library of Congress Control Number: 2023905607

Printed in the United States of America

10 9 8 7 6 5 4 3 2

Contents

Introduction

If you're seeking healing from the tragedies of everyday life, dealing with fake Felicia, toxic Taylor, and hatin' Hailey. You're in the right place. Yes, it does get better, but it starts with you. I must say, shit gets pretty real here; I'm an Aries so you could say I'm pretty direct. But, if you're serious about loving yourself and attracting greater things into your life, this is a book for you.

Before you start, get your mind flowing with the idea that anything is possible; remove the limits from your way of thinking. If you read with shackles on your mind, you will receive absolutely nothing from this. As I share my unique perspective of love and life, take what resonates with you.

You're here right now, this book is in your hands for a reason. Open yourself up to all the possibilities, get real, get comfortable, and dive in. Let's get started...

It all began when I decided to make the drastic change to go natural with my hair. That one little step of finally loving and accepting myself lead to a million other ways that have changed my life forever. Through this journey though long and at times stagnant I have been learning ways to love myself on a deeper level than I ever knew before. After diving deep into a state of solitude and truly embracing the meaning of pure unconditional love, I have recorded my dreams, created art, drowned myself in music, spilled my emotions and trials all on the pages several journals. Through it all I have transformed into a me that glows in even brighter than I thought possible. In this book I'd like to share some personal things I've learned so far on the way....

Dedicated to All My Sistas

Creating a new world starts with the transforming and healing of self. Through examining our reflection in nature we'll see, the basis of true growth begins at the roots. Which means healing the world starts with the metamorphosis of the women deepest in its origin.

Part 1: Love 101

We crave this thing we call love, but what the hell really is it? An emotion or an action? How many different kinds of love is there? Why is it so important? Where does it come from? How do we get it?

Chapter 1
Love vs Fear

"If you want to find the secrets of the universe think in terms of energy, frequency, and vibration."
    -Nikola Tesla | Inventor, Mechanical Engineer

Energy

The universe is full of energy; it is the make-up of everything around us. All of the energy making up the universe, including us, vibrates at a certain frequency. Frequency meaning, the rate or speed of a vibration that forms a wave. I think of it as energy everywhere constantly flowing like waves. They can move fast or slow. These waves flow through plants, animals, the atmosphere, humans, and materials etc. Although we can't physically see the waves, energy is everything. We all have energy vibrating throughout us.

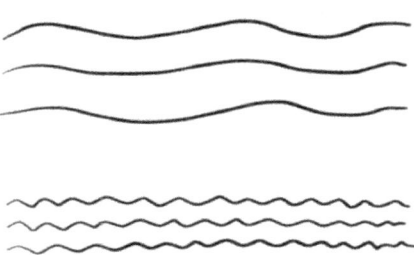

Human energy consists of different types; there's physical energy, emotional, mental, and spiritual. Our overall frequency depends on the vibrations of those types of energy. Fear being the lowest frequency and love being the highest.

Energy Attraction

We are all attracted to high frequency energy. Energy vibrating at a high frequency vibrates forms of **love**. Energy vibrating at a low frequency vibrates forms of **fear**. When we come in contact with a high frequency vibration we are attracted to it whether we consciously realize it or not. Our energy bodies are drawn to it. Ever met a person you are unexplainably attracted to? Just being around them makes you feel more alive. Their energy is vibrating at a high frequency and your energy is attracted to it. High frequency energy gives us a lighter feeling all over; more clarity, joy, and resilience in our being. Ever eaten fresh foods from the earth and felt really good afterward? Or had a bomb ass workout and felt lifted. Like your body feels revived; that's also energy. Whenever we vibrate at a high frequency we just feel good.

Even though we are all attracted to high frequency energy, the energy we attract to us is the energy we vibrate. I'm sure some of us have heard of the Law of Attraction; this is one of the laws of the universe. From my perspective, it's explaining how energy vibrating at a certain frequency attracts other energy vibrating at that same frequency. For example, when we create thoughts in our head of abundance and love, we are attracting abundance and love. If we create thoughts of lack and fear, we are attracting more lack and more fear.

"When you realize you're the most powerful magnet in the universe, attraction becomes your new superpower."
-Unknown

Visualize a bunch of energies everywhere, vibrating at different speeds. We're all just a bunch of radio stations; the ones tuning into the same frequency attract and stick together. Or think of it like a magnet; magnets are made up of the same electromagnetic field that pulls them together. When our energy is vibrating low, we will attract other low vibrating energy into our lives to exchange energy with. When our energy is vibrating high, we attract other energies vibrating just as high.

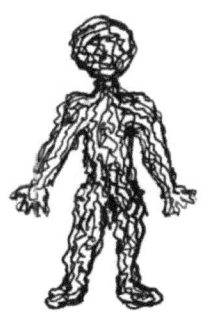

Not only does the energy we vibrate within our inner world matter, but the energy we put out in the things we do also attracts energy to us.

"Treat others how you want to be treated."

-Your Mom

All of us have heard this saying since we were kids; but, this quote goes so much deeper than we think. Treat everything how you want to be treated down to people, material objects, plants, animals, and career. Etc. The energy we put out toward those things always make its way back to us. Let's say you run a corrupt business; you constantly scam people for their money so you can have more. You're only attracting that back to you. Other low vibrations will flock to you because that is the energy you put out in the universe; career wise. Let's say you steal often; you might not get caught but you put an energy out into the universe of taking. The universe is going to match that by sending it back to you; you will constantly have things taken from you. This goes with everything; we are continuously offering the universe a vibration in various things we do and it is reflecting the same vibration back to us; mirroring. It may come back in a different form but it will always come back. Karma isn't really a bitch; she's you and she just plays fair. Put high vibrating energy out in all you do and watch it all come back to you. What you give you shall receive.

Energy Exchange

Every time we come in contact with other energies there is an exchange. Ever walked in a room full of sadness and suddenly started feeling sad yourself? These low vibrations have transferred to your energetic field and left you experiencing the same vibrations running throughout you. Energy never ends, it transfers until it is alchemized. Our energy flows to whatever we come in contact with and that energy flows to us (until we learn boundaries protection).

Unequal Energy Exchange

We have the power to raise our frequency. Once we do so, we also have the power to control the transfer of low frequency energy. When energy exchanges are unequal the higher vibrating energy will always feel less energy after the exchange. Think about it, we transfer our energy to it and it's to us. If ours is vibrating higher, we just gave a low vibration more energy and that low vibration gave us less.

If we run into low frequency energy we have control over how much thought we give, the emotions we give, and complete control over the actions we give toward the energy. Better yet, we can do our best to remove as many low frequency energies out of our life as we can. That way, there's limited exchange and the vibration of our energy can continue to rise.

Ever run into people who you can't quite put your finger on whether or not they are out to get you? Or people who make smart comments leaving you wondering, was that an insult? Even a place you get bad vibes from. Most of the time, the energy is trying to send a message to you; recognize it. To do this, we must practice becoming aware of low frequency energy around us. Trust your gut; energy never lies, we are energy.

Those environments which drain us, those people who suck the happiness right out of us, and those foods that leaves us with an extreme case of the itis; we have to become aware of them. It's hard to see the toxicity around us when we haven't been exposed to anything else or if we ignore the signs. I've been there before; I kept attracting the same people and situations into my life, but didn't understand why. I just thought this was life; so, continued to eat my feelings and suppress my emotions. This can become so drowning we aren't even aware of all the low vibrations building up in our present; we think it's normal. Becoming aware of it all becomes easier once we raise our own frequency, so we know when we are left feeling less.

Raising Our Frequency

Earlier, I mentioned human energy is made up of different parts; we have the ability to raise the vibrations of all of those. There's mental energy which includes things like; our own thoughts plus everything we see and hear. Physical energy; body movement and things we consume. Spiritual energy; authenticity, our passion, and purpose. Then, there's emotional energy; the feelings moving through us. Nourishing these energy bodies is how we raise our frequency. Just like there are four energy bodies there are four elements which create life as we know it; water, fire, air, and earth. Each of these elements align with one of our energy bodies. Water; emotional. Fire; spiritual. Air; mental. Earth; physical. All of these energy bodies are important to keep healthy for their own sake but also for the sake of each other. Although we have separate energy bodies which are their own vibration; they still act as a unit creating this life experience we have on earth. Meaning the vibrations of each affect each other.

Physical – Earth

Movement

I'm sure we've heard of all the benefits of exercise; getting the heart pumping and energy flowing. This flow picks up the speed of our physical vibration, raising the frequency. It's primitive we find something to move around and burn energy, however we choose to do this: yoga, running, dancing, biking, swimming, or kickboxing etc. When we stay active we can burn off low vibrating energy manifested within the physical body or simply move around stagnant energy in the body. All movement is beneficial and has an impact on our physical energy. Certain practices such as Tai Chi, Khemetic yoga, and belly dancing can also help activate certain energy points known as chakras: the flow of life force energy within us. Do these things out in the presence of nature for even more of a vibrational lift.

Nourishment

Equally as important; everything we consume affects our physical energy. The energies of the things we consume merge with our own energy; having an effect on the frequency. There are about 37 trillion cells in a living body. Each cell is a single living organism and necessary for a particular function in our body. These cells make up our entire being; we survive based on the health of these cells. These cells are also constantly making new ones; think of it like they are having new babies and the old ones are dying off. These newborn baby cells are made by the old ones metabolizing what we feed them. Basically, the things we eat are used as fuel to create the life of the new cells that rule our bodies. Our entire body functions exactly like the energy we feed it. Everything we eat and put on our bodies affects us on a much deeper level than we think. All of the energy we consume becomes an energy in us and goes down to the very core of us. What we eat becomes what we are; we get to choose what we're made of.

Remember, I mentioned our four energy bodies correspond with the four elements; fire, water, air, earth. Earth corresponds with our physical body; earth is our home just like our bodies are home to our soul. We must take care of both; starting with using earth to nourish our physical bodies. Although, a lot of us (including me) tend to attempt feeding our emotions with our food. Maybe we've had a bad day or just need a pick me up. So, we use food to make ourselves "feel good" in a non-physical way; hoping the taste of the food will satisfy our emotional bodies. We have to train ourselves in understanding food is for the nourishment of our physical body and not our emotions. Although I have had moments where I've just finished some fire ass SOL food and felt hella good after; physically and emotionally seeming too. I think food from mother earth does have the ability to affect our emotions in a pleasing way. Yet, I don't think it should be our main drive to eat. In my opinion it has to be a balance between eating to feel good physically and letting that satisfy us emotionally as well.

If we want to raise our frequency, we should consume energy rich foods. Energy rich meaning, things which are created from nature. We thrive off of Sol food; food from the earth nourished and grown with the help of the sun, water, and a conducive environment. Nature's food vibrates at high frequencies due to the energy needed from the sun, earth, air, and water to make it. The universe creates these foods from energies of itself. Which is the source of all energy. There's plenty of studies out there showing the amazing effects of consuming a highly plant based diet. Amazing things happen when nourish our body with high frequency energy; we feel lighter, vibrant, and overall our body functions more efficiently.

When we eat, the same energy transfers happen as when we come in contact with people. We don't want to transfer energy with things vibrating at very low levels. Personally, I refrain from consuming the very low energies of refined foods, genetically modified foods, pharmaceutical drugs, low quality meat, and dairy. Because one, it has an effect on my quality of life and two, it's all a system anyway. We buy foods designed to make us sick and need those pharmaceutical drugs. Those drugs temporarily cover up the symptoms, while causing more in other places of the body. So, we have to keep purchasing them in order to function, lead alone feel good; pharmaceuticals are a top money making industry. Why do you think there's only fast food restaurants, liquor stores, and pharmacies in the hood? It's just another form of enslavement.

There's a lot of foolishness going on and a lot of people making big bank; but, of course you're welcome to develop your own opinion. But I will hit you with some more facts; the soul food you thought I was talking about earlier, the one most familiar to the black community is food from slave days. Short Documentary: *The Post Traumatic Slave Diet* educates us on our diets before the slave trade and after.[13] When our ancestors were first taken away from the motherland and tossed onto the ships; they were fed slop made from red beans, cornmeal, pork fat, and other disregarded parts of the pig. Sound familiar? Many rejected this unfamiliar slop; those who did experienced removal of all front teeth and were force fed the slop through a tube. Many ate it out of starvation; it became the only food available for survival through the middle passage. When our ancestors were brought on land they were still given leftover scraps from the pig. Because we are so beautifully creative, our ancestors found a way to make all this junk taste mighty fire and passed down the recipes. So the soul food we know of today; chitterlings, pig's feet, red beans and rice, corn bread, and mac and cheese, is part of a *Post Traumatic Slave Diet*.[13] It was depreciating us then, its depreciating us now; only now we've come accustomed to it.

Additionally, I know we all love hot sauce; somehow it makes everything taste good. But think about it, if this is such a supported stereotype toward the black community, it can't be healthy. The average hot sauce has around 460 mg of sodium per tbsp. For a healthy salt to water ratio in the body, the American Heart association claims we should stay around 1,500 mg per day.[6] That's 3 tbsp of hot sauce and your done for the next 24 hours; and 3 tbsp. ain't nearly enough to sauce up the whole fried fish dinner, think about that. What we call soul food is low vibrational energy forced upon our culture by the oppressor. I know this is hard to hear but I'm willing to bet most of us don't want to intentionally exchange energy with toxicity. I'm not telling everyone they immediately need to go fully plant based; your lifestyle is your choice. But, keep in mind when we consume animals or animal produce we consume their energy. If those animals were tortured, injected, and living in filth, we consume those energies of pain, fear, anxiety, and depression they've felt their entire lives. When we eat pain, we feel pain. When we eat anxiety, we feel anxiety. When we eat depression, we feel depression. Whether it shows up as physical, emotional, or mental pain, the energy is still transferring to ours. The life in flesh dies, but the physical body which is still energy is what we are consuming. I can say from personal experience, anxiety lessens when we stop consuming it. Nature is calm, peaceful, and present.

Not only are we consuming the energy of pain, we consume whatever food those animals have been fed. Which most of the time is full course meal of corn accompanied with a side of shit from its peers; literal shit, like feces. Even if the animals were grass fed and free roaming, we are still eating dead flesh and not live energetic foods. If you think about it, humans are on some zombie type shit; we eat dead rotting flesh. Not even freshly killed flesh like real carnivores. At least real carnivorous animals eat their meat warm off the bone. We let it sit, travel from factory to store, let it sit in the fridge a little longer, and then cook it creating carcinogens.

Just like when us humans die, the body immediately starts to rot. Unless pumped full of formaldehyde and other chemicals to preserve it. My question is, how many and what chemicals are being used to preserve dead animal flesh until it gets onto our plates? Okay, let's take a breath. I'm not exactly saying we should never eat anything from an animal ever again. Our Indigenous ancestors occasionally consumed animal protein. But, there was a a ceremony; a ritual performed before kill the animal to give gratitude and respect. Ultimately to give gratitude for the transitions of those animal's qualities to our own being instead of consuming fearful vibrations left behind from experiencing a tragic death. The industry is completely different now. It's about capital, not health.

We eat energy; it's us who decides what type we take in. Every time we consume something we are either giving more life to a disease or taking its power; eat to live! Raise your frequency by changing your diet. The type of food we've become accustomed to is what's destroying us; it's not the food our Afakan ancestors ate long before slavery which created the Afrakan genome; our incredible genetic makeup. They ate sol food, electric food from the sun and we must return to these ways. Dr. Alfredo Bowman, aka Dr. Sebi, a healer and herbalist who has successfully cured a variety of diseases with an alkaline plant based reminds us of the importance of returning to mother nature for overall healing of the whole self.[5]

"Fruits for electricity, vegetables for grounding, herbs for healing, and nuts and seeds for building."
-    **Dr. Alfredo Bowman | Herbalist & Healer**

Topical Consumption

Things we put in are equally as important as things we put on our body. Our skin is our largest organ; its commonly said that 60% of what we put on it is absorbed into our bloodstream within 26 seconds. This is for adults; children absorb even a higher percentage of what's put on the skin. The consumer good industry has convinced us we need to buy all sorts of cosmetic products on the market to keep our skin and hair prospering. The gag is, Europe has banned around 1,300 chemicals which are commonly used in cosmetics; the U.S. has only banned 30.[14] Not to mention, some say the Federal Chemical Safety has not been updated since 1976. Which means majority of the most popular brands used today are flooded with poisonous chemicals such as Parabens, Polyethylene Glycols (PEG's), and Phthalates; which are endocrine disrupting chemicals which can later cause skin rashes and irritation, reproductive harm, birth defects, and even cancer. Even more for women; the beauty industry sells us the idea of beauty coming from the outside. So, we're quick to purchase whatever new beautifying product is on the market; without considering what's in it.

Dr. Mercola, an alternative medicine professional, studies have shown, on average, women absorb five pounds of toxic chemicals per year from makeup, skin, hair, and all sorts of hygiene products.[11] Imagine how much five pounds of toxicity is lowering our vibration. Everything is energy; these heavy and low vibrations are making us weaker and pumped full of fear. In my opinion, this can't be a coincidence; society has placed women in positions below men in politics, education, and finance. Why wouldn't they purposely place us in a lower energy to further support the so called superiority of men? I'll cover more on color energies later; but, for now I'll share with you this fun fact; while absorbing the energy of the color pink, the human body is physically weakened. Just a food for thought. Anyhow, us women think we have to buy all sorts of makeup and other products to fit society's beauty standards. When in reality, the chemicals in these products are diminishing our energy, beauty, health, and slowly depreciating the money in our wallets. For me I used to think in order to be beautiful I had to conform to European standards. So, I started getting relaxers to make my hair straight. Little did I know, relaxers are straight up toxic chemicals. I don't know about ya'll, but when I got my relaxers those burning ass chemicals sat on my scalp for well over 26 seconds. Which means over 60% of those chemicals found their way into my bloodstream. Every 6 weeks for 7 years, I was being pumped full of toxic chemicals. That's only through one stream. You're probably thinking whew chile this is a lot. But, we didn't even discuss flu shots, new born vaccinations, bleached tampons, or toxic cleaning products. More toxins we're being conditioned to fill our bodies with from the moment we arrive to this planet. Ultimately to lower our vibration and prevent self-actualization by controlling and enslaving our physical energy without us being conscious of it.

Earth is how we heal externally and internally. The only way we will truly thrive inside and out is from the nourishment of mother nature. We can avoid using chemically filled products by monitoring the ingredients in our everyday toothpaste, moisturizers, deodorant, perfume, hair products, and makeup. To keep our vibration high, return to the beautifying recipes of our ancestors. Exchange energy with a variety of healing plants, herbs, and essential oils on the skin. There is a natural remedy for everything; we have cocoa butter, charcoal, coconut oil, argan oil, clay, rose water, and so much more! There are tons of homemade beauty recipes out there and even tons of high quality brands selling truly natural products. Either way, whether we choose to gather our own ingredients or support other clean beauty businesses, earth provides everything we possibly need. Nature enhances our physical energy. #Naturalisthewaytoglow

Why is This So Important?

When low vibrations within us are left untreated, they manifest into aches, pains, illnesses, and diseases. Frequency is measured in hertz, which represent how many waves pass each second. The inventor and builder of the first frequency monitor Bruce Tainio, discovered disease begins at 58 MHz, cancer begins at 42 MHz, and death starts at 25 MHz.[1] If we continue to lower our vibration within our physical energy, our bodies get sick, and eventually shut down. Disease runs in families because it's all energy, frequency, and vibrations. Our children are made from our DNA; our physical, mental, emotional, and spiritual energy is what creates them. Those same low vibrations within us will pass down to our children and theirs until the frequency is raised. Our frequency is directly connected to our quality of life; let's start healing by consuming high vibrating, earthly, and life force plants within our physical energy body. Tupac told us in his song *Changes*, we have to change the way we eat and the way we live to start making changes within the world.[16]

Transitioning

Filling the physical body with nature is a lifestyle change; meaning a quick overnight fix isn't going to happen. Keep in mind, we are reprogramming ourselves to cut out food we've been eating our whole lives. Food our mothers ate; which made us in the wound. Many of our bodies are made from the energies of these GMO toxic foods we've been fed, so it's no surprise we will crave these things during the transition; like attracts like. Which is why I always recommend slowly eliminating things from your diet and surroundings. Do your own research, have patience with yourself, and trust what works for you. Whether you choose to change a few things or completely transform your entire lifestyle, whatever you incorporate opens up a new layer of glow within you.

Personally, I started with my hair. I began embracing my natural hair by loving and nourishing it. With the addition of natural hair came tons of exploring ways to treat it properly. All the research on natural hair lead to learning the benefits of incorporating nature in our bodies. The hair process by itself was super long for me. Figuring out what worked for my hair, what routine to stick with, what my hair hates, and what it loves. There were definitely some fallbacks as well. I dyed my hair, damage it, and ended up cutting it several times before I truly got in my mojo. Even now I'm still always trying new things with it. While in the process of converting to natural hair my interest also tipped over into skin care. The new knowledge I learned of using nature lead me to believe natural is best for more than just hair. I studied more about ingredients; what's in skincare and how our skin truly thrives. I learned the importance of nourishing the melanin in my skin. I also tried a ton of DIY (do it yourself) recipes for my hair and skin. After a while I started noticing a huge difference; I looked healthier. Looking healthy gave me a glow I had never seen in myself before; but, I wanted to do more than just look healthy, I wanted to be healthy inside and out. So, I started slowly changing my diet. First, it was just getting rid of processed foods, junk food, and fast food. Which was way harder than I thought; honestly for me my internal diet was the hardest transition of all. It took me years to stay consistent; being in high school and college, plus maintaining a healthy diet is hard as hell. For a period of time I would eat super healthy, then I would relapse and binge eat my entire kitchen. I remember a time I went to Red Lobster and ate about 20 biscuits plus my entire meal. Then ate 5 burgers at a grad party; shit happens. When transitioning it's crucial to know we will encounter fallbacks and there's nothing wrong with that; failure is our teacher. If we eat something we wish we didn't, just start again the next day. I can't even count how many cheat days I've had and I'm not ashamed of it. Truthfully, the beginning transition was so difficult I had more than just cheat days; it was cheat weeks, months, and even a year. My entire freshman year in college sent my health down the drain. But we're all human and we are surrounded by food propaganda daily; the amount of self-love and self-control it takes to eliminate things we've been accustomed to our whole lives must be built up over time. Know it's not about never eating unhealthy food or never messing up; it's about consistency which means never giving up.

Because I learned from my mistakes, continued educating myself, and never gave up, I was able to keep transitioning. After about 4 years of trying to figure this healthy shit out, I made a switch to a pescatarian diet for about 6 months. After those six months I began slowing down the sea food and cutting out all dairy for the remainder of the year. After another year or so, I was able to convert to a mostly plant based diet from then on.

It all started with my hair and over a span of 6 years I've been slowly eliminating things to live in the highest vibration I can. To nourish myself in every way possible. Transitioning to natural hair, vegetarian, nontoxic, plant based or natural anything are all huge life changes which take time to adjust. There's a lot of physical adjustments as the cells in our body need to regenerate. Personally, my body went through major changes. With the shift in my diet, there was a huge amount of weight loss and craving in the beginning. There were times when I thought this lifestyle wasn't sustainable for my body. But, the more I stuck with it, my body started to regulate. I reached my normal body weight again, my taste buds completely transformed, and eventually things I once craved, no longer sounded appetizing. Now, my cells are accustomed to the energy I feed them; I feel as if I'm nourished with everything I need. It takes constant reconditioning and learning of new information to succeed.

The transition becomes easier once we balance the patience and slow progress with sustainable motivation and mind power. By sustainable motivation I mean getting to the real root of why we should change. Not to lose weight or ride the natural trend, but to truly show ourselves love. Truth, health, longevity, and high vibration is the motivation. We have to love ourselves enough to want these things and believe we can have them before we successfully transition to high frequency physical energy. Then, to really light a fire under that ass we need will power which comes from mind control. Start by turning off the fast food commercials telling your brain a McChicken is a delicious meal. Tell yourself you can change; you don't need those foods. The real power comes from the mind. It's in control of the physical energy body. When you have mind control and connection to the physical body, your body will begin to tell your mind what you need instead of the outside world.

Activity

The mixing pot = My body.

Review these questions.

1. What all did I eat today and what was in it?
2. What did I put on my skin today and what was in it? (lotion, perfume, deodorant, makeup, soap etc.)
3. If I were to put all the ingredients of what I ate today and what I put on my skin in one large mixing pot, what type of energy will I have created? Toxicity or nourishment?

Mental – Air/ Atmosphere

Air literally meaning oxygen. We need oxygen to thrive which means focusing on our breath work. We often forget to do the most basic component of life; breath. Especially when accompanied by fear. Practice breathing techniques to raise your frequency. I've had personal experiences where anxiety aka the voice in the back of my head that's a devil on my shoulder, starts pouring thoughts into my head. These thoughts cloud my mental energy with low vibrations and sometimes I become a victim of them. But, I've realized, all I have to do is breathe. Take deep breaths in and out; it's like the air I breathe inward comes to sweep up all those worrisome thoughts. Then I blow them all out, replacing the space I just cleaned up with higher vibrating ones.

Thoughts

The words I am, I can, and I will have so much power; words are energy too. So, when all the motivational speeches tell us to begin reading affirmations, inspiring books, and checking our thoughts, listen. Our own thoughts are so important to keep in check. Not only does our body listen to everything the mind tells it; our mind creates this illusion we call reality.

Since we create our own illusion of reality within our mind, every time we think a thought we open up an entirely new illusion full of whatever possibilities our mind allows.

To keep our mental energy vibrating high and harness the ability to create a magical illusion, we need our imagination. Remember when we were kids and had nothing to play with? Our parents told us, "use your imagination", and so we did. We made up tons of songs, games, dances, and other activities to keep us busy. Turns out, our parents helped us develop a crucial habit; this use of mind power is incredibly magical.

"Imagination is the air of the mind."
-Phillip James Bailey | Poet, Author

We'll touch up more on the power of the thoughts throughout the book.

Sight

What we see has an impact on our energetic field. To keep our mental energy vibrating high, we should consider how much time we spend on social media and who we follow. Not that social media is a bad thing, it's a really powerful tool. Since it's such a powerful tool and a part of a lot of our everyday lives; it has an impact on us. All the photos, tweets, captions, and statuses we view are a determining factor in our mental energy. It's important to monitor what type of energy in our social media we are allowing ourselves to be exposed to.

Another way we can vibrate higher in our mental body is to create an atmosphere that suits us. Colors in our environment have an effect on our energy; what we're seeing is light energy of different frequencies. The human eye can only see a fraction of all the light frequencies; *The Minds Journal*, a digital mental health journal, says it equates to about 430-770 tHz.[8] This is the red to violet color spectrum: red, orange, yellow, green, blue, indigo, violet. The same seven colors we see when nature creates a rainbow from light. Violet being the highest vibration red being the lowest. This doesn't mean red is a color we should avoid; all of these colors are made from light, meaning their vibrations are of high energy. It's the lack of color we have to look out for.

Once upon a time, my bedroom was filled with all black everything; black bedding, rugs, and wall décor. I wondered why I found it so hard to wake up in the morning. Why the fresh new day wasn't enough to give me the energy I needed. Then, I realized I was cocooning in a black hole all night. As soon as I removed some of the black and added pops of bright color; my vibration changed and in exchange, so did my reality. The same way we exchange energy with people and foods we do with colors. Not only the colors in our environment but the ones even closer to us; the colors we wear on our bodies affect us as well. If we want to raise our energy with colors, we can study what types of energies they carry. The seven colors I mentioned earlier are in tune with the seven energy points in our body, also known as chakras. We can wear certain colors to activate certain energies associated with each chakra. Wear red for grounding; root chakra. Wear orange if you're feeling sensual or creative; sacral chakra. Wear yellow if you want to be bright and confident; solar plexus chakra. Then, green or pink for love; heart chakra. Blue for expression; throat chakra. Finally, wear purple and white for meditating; crown chakra (We'll understand chakras more later). On top of color therapy, we can surround ourselves with plants, inspiring words, sunlight or anything we see that gives us good vibes.

Sound

Just like the human eye can only see a fraction of light frequency, the human ear can only detect a certain range of sound frequencies; which is between 20Hz-20 kHz.[8] These frequencies we can see and hear are only a small fraction of total light and sound; which means there's a lot energy around us we can't even mentally process; without the help of psychedelics or spiritual work. These higher frequency sounds aren't easy to hear for humans but for nature and animals; the sound is probably clear. Reasons why dog whistles are silent to us, but loud and clear to dogs and other animals. I believe the higher our frequency the more we can tune in with the high pitch sounds out of normal sound range. Anyhow, the seven color frequencies we can see (rainbow) line up with the seven notes in music as well as the 7 chakras. These sound frequencies are notes we call a, b, c, d, e, f, and g. Need I say again; everything is energy. What we hear has an impact on our energy. If we choose to listen to music, it's important to truly look into what we're soaking up. Music notes and lyrics are energies. We've all had those moments where we catch ourselves singing the lyrics of a song we don't even like; just because we've heard it so many times. Those words stick with us in our mental energy. For me, music is a huge part of my daily life. When I realized the lyrics I constantly listened to were becoming a part of me, I began paying a lot closer attention to the type of lyrics in my playlist. These lyrics had a space in my mental energy, affecting the way I think and act. Of course music isn't the only thing we hear; what we watch on Tell-a-Vision, listen to podcasts, and talk about with others can either lower or raise our frequency.

Reconstructing Mental Programming

To raise the vibration of our mental energy we have to not only make changes to our present atmosphere, but also commit to healing and reconstructing the things we've already seen and heard. Creating love within is about reconstructing fear based thoughts and beliefs we have developed in our life.

What we see and hear from society concerning us with melinated skin is almost never positive. We all know how this goes; news forecast shows the worst picture they can find of a man who has supposedly committed a crime; they highlight negative habits and behaviors all to portray a certa n image. Through a variety of ways we see and hear, we've been trained to picture all our men as thugs; only good for trouble and danger. When a black man comes around it's no wonder why purses are clutched; where do you think people have developed that fear from? It's not often black men are portrayed as intelligent, protective, talented, and strong human beings. The oppressor and even us as a people tend to feed and broadcast the shadow aspects over the Godliness of black men and women. All of this conditioning of mental energy only comes back to bite everyone in the ass; creating no peace for anyone. Pac told us again when he said Thug L fe, all low vibrations society places in the minds of kids growing up; the portrayed images in the news, the school system etc. etc. etc., ends up fucking with everyone.

Additionally, many reality Tell-a-Vision shows – Wait PAUSE; T.V. is literally a distraction which tells a certain vision to a mass of people. It's a power move; it uses all of our free time when our minds are idle and open to new ideas. Then, creates an image within which projects in our reality. The T.V. takes up our mental space for us so we don't have the power to project our own high vibration or control our mental energy (which is super important to have btw). Not saying we shouldn't watch T.V. all, because movie nights with friends are lit and there are meaningful shows out there. Just be mindful of how long and often our eyes are glued to any type of screen and what we are absorbing.

Back to where we were, T.V. shows continue to portray us black women as one who seeks drama and bickers constantly. Black women arguing is nothing new to the television screen. We've been mental y programmed to flat out disrespect and disregard black women because of the image we have in our minds. We've been conditioned to lack appreciation, judge, and project fear onto the black woman in many different ways. For the purpose of how others view us and how we view ourselves. To enslave our minds, control us, and blind us from seeing the immense depth and sacredness of the melanin womban . Although we birthed the entire human race but I'll sip my tea on that in this book. A good amount of mainstream hip hop has gone from a creative way to teach empowerment, to music which has us believing women are only objects to strip in the background of the music videos. Frank Ocean tries to show us the evolution in perception of the Afrakan Queen in his song *Pyramids*; from worshipped Cleopatra to working at the pyramid only useful for bringing home paper for big daddy.[12] Society has ruined the perception us men and women have of each other through mental conditioning. Not to mention the education system never speaks about Afrakans before slavery; a huge chunk of history missing. Like always, there's a reason. This is only a small piece of the programming; it runs deeper than what we see and hear.

Not only has modern day mentality infected the minds of us black folk. History has already planned to mentally fuck us for generations. Though the *Willy Lynch Letter* is very controversial I believe in the planned programming of slaves it speaks on.[10] The letter mentions all the beatings, killings, and ways of speech around the slaves had purpose. I'll briefly share a couple. The conditioning of the light skin vs dark skin is one most are familiar with. Our status, worth, and beauty was measured by the tone of our skin. A brutal method mentioned in the letter was the act of men being set on fire, burned alive, and torn apart limb from limb in front of their wife and children; this being to program the woman's mind to be independent despite her man, because he could not protect her from the oppressor. Also, enforcing women to raise the children in opposite roles; the young girls primarily in their masculine energy as solely providers, leaders, and protectors of the children and the young boys in their feminine energy as endangered and fragile beings in fear of their lives. These programming techniques were meant to last 300 plus years by spreading from generation to generation through DNA. As DNA is energy and also records behavior. Though these conditioned behaviors and ideas were planned to last for hundreds of years, these masterminds know conditioning is not permanent. In order to keep control of the minds, conditioning must be reinforced. The letter was supposedly written around the beginning of the

1700's. Which marks the 2000's as reinforcement time. Aka, men getting shot dead by law enforcement in front of their wife and kids, raised in fear of their lives. Also, the rising concept of women being so fiercely independent they need no one, causing us to subconsciously reject the idea community and universal equation of partnership with the black man. Then, the booming reality T.V. shows featuring black women in competition regarding appearance and status. All to keep our minds controlled.

We can see how fast media and technology is expanding. A video shot all the way across the world can easily be viewed right in our bedroom. This being used to aid in reinforcement. How many videos do we see of innocent black lives being taken away? We absorb visuals of spilled blood from black and brown bodies in movies, the news, and social media. This way, we don't have to experience it in real life to have those visuals burned in our mental energy. These visuals can affect everyone now. Whether it shows up as anger, resentment, or rage, it's all a vibration of fear. Ultimately these low vibrating emotions we carry toward something stem from fear of that something or a situation similar appearing into our reality. Fear of being pulled over, locked up, or killed. Going back to the law of energy attraction, the things we are fearful of, we carry the vibration and we attract that situation or one similar. There are things we're conditioned to fear so we attract those scenarios. You feel me? We have to free ourselves from survival mode. We move and make decisions based on fear when our mind is focused on survival.

If you ask me, this shit is working pretty effectively; it's still very visible today. The crazy thing is these are only very few of the thought out programming ideas mentioned in the letter; the list goes on. The generational tradition in colored families not mentioned is the idea of spanking children as a form of discipline. So yes, other cultures do participate in spanking their children when they act up. But, if you know you know; us black kids get our asses beat with hands, belts, switches, lamps, tree branches, and just about anything laying around at the time.

26

Like all human actions, this has been mentally ingrained in us. Our ancestors were beat by slave masters as a form of discipline; we are repeating the cycle with our children. In several ways we are mentally enslaved. With the education of reprogramming of our mental energy we can finally realize our power.

From personal experience, things got a lot lighter after I cleaned up my head space. It took time and effort to truly detox my mental energy and start controlling my own thoughts. I will say, monitoring everything on the outside really helped with understanding the inside. The reason why our mental energy corresponds with air is because our atmosphere affects our mental energy. If we want to raise the frequency within our minds, we must check our atmosphere.

Our body has over 37 trillion cells; these cells listen to everything the mind tells it. Each cell is its own living organism; so, think of our body like a community full of life; our mind being the government in charge of this community. Whatever this powerful government thinks affects our taste buds, body movements, logic, opinions, and beliefs. Ask yourself, how are the things in my atmosphere affecting what I communicate to my cells? Our mind is an extremely powerful tool just like a government; it creates our reality. Take charge and create the environment you want to live in.

Activity 1

Let's take a look.

- List your top 10 favorite songs. What are they saying?

- List your top 5 favorite TV shows. What are they about?

- Scroll down your social media, list the top 10 topics your followers are talking/posting about.

- Look at your list and ask yourself, are these words, videos, pictures, and lyrics lowering or raising my vibration? Are they creating love or fear within me?

- Do some detoxing.

Activity 2

Reality Check

1. Who are the 5 people you spend most of your time with? List them. "If you fuck around with a fuck around you'll fuck around and get fucked around with." -Unknown

Ask yourself these questions when you get to each name.

1. Does this person match my energy after I tell them good news?

2. Have I ever questioned if this person is truly happy for me?

3. Is this person adding to or subtracting from my energy? (fear or love)

4. How does this person make me feel when I'm around them and when I leave? (motivated, insecure, lazy, unimportant, sketchy, etc.)

Activity 3

Affirmations

1. Write down at least **least** 30 affirmations such as:
    - I love myself.
    - I take care of myself mentally, physically, spiritually, and emotionally.
    - I create my reality and I fill it with unconditional love.

2. Play soothing instrumentals or nature sounds in the background and voice record yourself saying these affirmations in the present tense. Listen to this recording every night while falling asleep to program the subconscious mind.

Emotional – Water

Our mind is how we use logic; how we make sense of everything we know to be true. Our emotions have no logic, emotional energy is feminine energy with movement and flow; it is energy moving through us. Just like water, emotional energy is deep and powerful enough to drown us or help us float on top of life; feeling free and alive. This all depends on the frequency of our emotional body. When we have no control over our emotions and we let them sit in us and pile up they can start to make us feel heavy causing us to drown in our own sorrows. Yet, when we let emotions move through us and release them, we operate in a lighter state, allowing us to float. Emotional energy is connected to water for several reasons. It acts just as water; flowing, deep, powerful, and feminine. Water also helps us cleanse us which also raises our energy. When we take baths and submerge ourselves in water; the element can not only cleanse our physical form but help cleanse us of low vibrations in our emotional body. It can bring to the surface whatever emotions we are feeling and allow us to let go. Then, there are our tears which are made of salt water; another way we release emotional energy.

People with a lot of water signs in their astrology chart feel their emotions a lot stronger as a oose to other signs. Pisces, Cancer, and Scorpio signs are extremely emotional beings who love being around water because those signs are the element of water. Hopefully you can see how things are aligning. In my full astrological chart water holds a very small space. Emotional energy is different for me. It took deeper lessons for me to understand the power of our emotional energy body and how to raise the frequency. We'll talk about it in depth in a later chapter; diving into that lesson is deep, so be ready for it.

Spiritual – Fire

A healthy mental space by itself, cannot completely nourish our being. Just like a nourished body, won't solve all of life's issues. It is the balance of mind, body, emotion, and spirit; air, earth, water, and fire that create the harmonious equilibrium of life.

"It's hard to be happy when your spirit is hungry."

-Michael Todd | Husband, Father, Pastor

From how I see things I believe our spiritual energy is already a high vibration because of how deep and close it is to the soul; but, we can help those vibrations come alive by being in alignment with our true self and getting in touch with our creative will. We have to get to know our true selves before we can fully love ourselves. Which means living authentically, acting in our passion, and serving our purpose in this world. Doing the things that set a fire in us is what's going to feed our spirit. To truly listen to our spirit and find those deeper connections, we can practice prayer and meditation; a way to connect with ourselves and our source. This stillness helps us get in touch with our raw spirit and truest desires. The ones deep deep down; covered up by the noise of the world and our ego. Meditation can help us listen to the whispers of our spirit which will guide us in every decision we need to make to be in perfect alignment with our life's path.

"Be still. Stillness reveals the secrets of eternity."

– Lao Tzu | Chinese Philosopher

Meditation is conscious connection with spirit, while sleep is like unconscious meditation. When we enter a deep sleep we are submerged in our own truth and nothingness. Our spirits nature can just be. Were no longer sustaining in the physical realm; our bodies rest while our spirit is nourished with whatever energy we encounter in the spiritual. We get to go to dreamland; where our spirit can speak to us through projected images and symbols to guide us when we return to waking life. To keep our spiritual energy healthy, we need sleep; so, embrace the stillness. Then, when the darkness of the night has passed absorb the sunlight. Our spiritual energy connects with the element of fire. The sun is a big ass ball of fire, so it will nourish our spiritual energy and raise our frequency when we absorb it. Even Ancient Afrakans worshipped the sun as a spiritual practice; hence the reason for the sun kissed skin in our DNA. If you lock at the sun long enough you'll be able to see it is a perfect circle; the rays which shine and light up the entire world is it's aura, its own energy which creates light in and around it. Light is high vibrating energy. When we vibrate high we carry an aura which brings light everywhere we go like the sun; we are the sun. Our high vibrational energy brightens other's day, makes them feel warm, and most importantly does those things for us.

Like fire, spiritual energy is much more profound and intense. I believe it is the deepest energy within our human form; the closest energy to our actual soul which is the immortal god like energy we truly are. So, we have to nourish our sacred spiritual energy; nourish it ourselves and exchange high vibrating energy with others. A deep spiritual energy exchange happens when we are intimate with others and when we express the depth of our spirit. This can be joined creation, mediation, prayer, or sex etc. We can exchange spiritual energy with others in different ways but sex is a huge one. It is the merging and exchange of spiritual, mental, physical, and emotional energy; every element that makes the soul human. It's powerful; it's the energy which magically creates a human life. Anyhow while having sex, the low or high vibrations of each person will now become a part of the other. Like we are deeply connected or tied to that person.

A lot of people go out and have sex to feed insecurities. Let's be real for a second. Some men pour out their feelings of fear, inadequacy, and lack of masculinity into a woman for a feeling of conquer. Thinking it makes them more masculine because it makes women vulnerable to them.

Then, there are some women who exchange their low self-esteem and lack of self-worth for a moment of affection, distraction, and acceptance. Now in days where the hook up culture is exploding, sex tends to be an exchange of low vibrational energies. We have to remember it's not just a physical thing; it's spiritual. We begin to emulate all of what has been exchanged in our sacred energy. So we must fully consider who we let in our deepest parts.

"Study their ingredients before feeding them to your soul."

-Unknown

Am I saying we must only have sex with one person or we must wait until marriage? Not at all; we are naturally sexual beings and we must embrace that. Whether you decide to wait, have few, many, or multiple partners at once. All I'm saying is listen to spirit; you know what's truly best for you to have healthy sexual and spiritual energy. When a sexual desire rises ask yourself is this my spirit asking me to merge with another or is this my ego needing to be fed? Could this be my body craving momentary pleasure? Could this be pressure from society to conform to what's on trend? Could this be my emotions needing a distraction? Am I opening myself up to receiving toxic energy or life force energy? Sex is a powerful tool that should be used to imprint high vibrational energy from both sides. It is so power, it's the energy that creates life. When it is abused, it can be toxic.

Ever been in a relationship with a toxic Taylor, whom you shared your complete human energy with? The breakup finally happens and we think we're free. Then, terrific Terri comes around and rocks our world again. Later, we come to find who we thought was terrific Terri is exactly like toxic Taylor. It is because the low frequency vibrations of toxic Taylor are still vibrating in us. Until we begin healing and releasing those mental, emotional, physical, and spiritual energies from Taylor, we will continuously attract more Toxic Taylors name Terri, Tony, and T.J. When we heal and shift our energy to vibrate high we will finally attract tantalizing Tyler (pun intended). Some of us have made choices to let the toxicity of others in; some of our spirits have been vandalized without our consent. Both require deep internal healing; healing and cleansing our own spiritual energy.

Sexual energy is very much a part of healing; many of us aren't aware we can still express this energy in so many other ways besides sexual intercourse with another being. We can dance, create art, feel every energy in our own being, and admire our own beautiful bodies; not just those of others. Connection is how we heal; it's one of the many beautiful things in life. So we must embrace it. Yet, we must connect with ourselves first, before we can make healthy connections with others.

Vibrating at a High Frequency

When our energy is vibrating high our well-being, desires, beliefs, environment, and social circle will begin to shift. A wise guy told me, if you have a lot of snakes in your life, your living too low. When you aim higher and follow your path toward greatness the snakes will disappear because snakes cannot survive in the high altitude. The higher we vibrate we'll notice we aren't as heavily consumed by hate, jealousy, pessimism, low self-esteem, or other forms of fear. Then, other people consumed by those low vibrations won't be attracted to us. They can see us, but they can't touch us.

There's work done by Dr. Bruce Lipton showing our current perceptions and beliefs can alter our genetics.[9] What we are currently thinking, believing, feeling, hearing, and seeing is changing the chemistry of our blood; our DNA. Which is changing our entire reality. The high frequency energy we are vibrating will begin to manifest the reality we desire. When our frequency is high we are a magnet for love, abundance, creativity, and flow.

"The universe does this thing where it aligns you with people, things, and situations that match our vibration. The higher our vibration the more we'll attract things that are beneficial to our wellbeing."

-Unknown

We Are Love

All things we can see, hear, touch, and taste are made up of energy vibrating at a certain frequency; we know this already. Studies have been done where certain frequencies were played and when next to solid matter, the matter arranged itself in a unique geometrical patterns which reflect that frequency. Exact patterns showing up multiple times through nature, humans, and animals; all living energies. These geometric patterns match things like the shapes on a leopard's body and a turtle's shell, the spirals in flowers, and the hexagons on bee hives. All of the universe is an energy vibrating at a certain frequency showing up in the material world as a color, physical matter, sound, and shape etc. The life running through these energies; what makes them grow, move,   and eat, just like us, is God. A single consciousness revealing itself in all living things. The life force running through all life in the universe; plants, animals, sun, and us. We are all energy with life force running through us. We are all one collective consciousness; small fractals of the life force energy appearing in solid form, seeming different but all the same. We are all an extension of God, love, and high frequency energy; we are a soul which is pure light. Our soul is the driver of these four elements; earth, air, water, and fire which we create our reality as a human on earth.

"The soul is the same in all living creatures, although the body of each is different."

-Hippocrates | Greek Physician

We have a connection with the universe/God/life force because that's what we are. All we have to do is tap into our true essence. Which means we must start with ourselves. The best way to stay vibrating at a high frequency is staying connected to God, universe, or whatever you vibe with. I'll switch it up through the book; so if I say God, universe, spirit, or higher power, know I'm referring to the same energy. Regardless of what we call it; it is the source of all energy. It is all around us and it is very real. The highest frequency is LOVE. God is love, love is light, love heals a l, love always wins, we all crave love, and we all need love.

In order to stay connected to our source of energy we must connect to it in all ways given to us as a human. Think of it like we have four different bodies; we have to check in on, cleanse, and nourish each one. Life is about balance; keeping our mental, spiritual, physical, and emotional energy vibrating in love as much as we can. Don't neglect others and focus on one, focus on all. When we focus on all we have **self-love**.

Chapter 2
SELF-LOVE

Proud

Pleasure and satisfaction in one's own achievements or qualities

High opinion in oneself or someone associated

See, my people were the first here from the world created

Blessed with wisdom by the God Source that made it

Studying life's purpose and dissecting the land

Out of nature came the man and womban

Working to create a life

Connecting to the energy of the light

Nourished with nature's medicine

Made strong through what we take in

Searing sun rays and exposed skin

Create the pigment called melanin

Gifted through genetic origin

Responsible for our beautiful brown skin

Heat causes a reaction to shrink

The reason for every curl and kink

On the heads of those with Afrakan links

These features are a symbol of knowledge and strength

At an unmeasurable length

Existence without a machine or a trigger

The reason for our breast, hips, and curvy figure

Muscle expands the more frequently used

When creating a civilization for existence, you would give it all wouldn't you?

So, take pleasure in nature's sunscreen

Let your skin be seen

Never restrain from loving your hair

Even if they stare

A proud king and queen do not care

Take time to consider why they do

To transform the generation to another version of you

But you are you

A work of art

A muse

Inspiration for others to know what to do

When I say be proud

Understand everything is inside of you

Strength, love, beauty, and virtue

Your beautiful roots affirm your identity

End the comparison and say

"I love me"

PROUD | Tyler A. Norman

What is Self-Love?

When we do face mask, bubble baths, and read affirmations; yes, all of those things are self-love. A few ways to make us feel good; but, self-love is truly so much deeper then we often realize. Self-love is when we shift our focus to taking care of our mental, physical, emotional, and spiritual energy. It's a mix between self-mastery and having patience for things unresolved. It's when we make it our number one priority to put our energy on top of the to-do list. Self-love is an infinite journey.

"Your task is not to seek for love, but merely to seek and find all the barriers within yourself that you have built against it."

-Rumi | Poet

I've always been told, love your neighbor as you love yourself. However, I didn't understand the true meaning. I couldn't act on it because I really didn't get it. Love your neighbor as you love yourself. So, exactly the way we love ourselves is how we should love our neighbor? As I began exploring the aspect of self-love on an even deeper level I've gained a new interpretation of this teaching. The way I see it, it's instinctively the exact love we have for ourselves is the love we will have for everyone around us; aka our neighbors. **The amount of love we feel in ourselves is the only** amount of love we can show and feel from others and the only amount they can show us. If we don't have love for ourselves how can we possible show love to someone else? Long story short we can only experience love on the outside as much as we have love on the inside. So, if we want a life full of love in many ways, we have to start from within.

"If you keep avoiding self-love, the universe will keep sending people who avoid loving you."

-Unknown

Creating Love Within

Most of us have an acute desire to receive some external form of love to fill us within. That's okay, we were all born with holes we need to fill up. We go into a relationship looking to get our holes filled by another person doing the same. Or, we buy a bunch of material things to bring us joy. We might even move from state to state in search of feeling full of something. The thing we have to realize is, our relationships and possessions aren't there to complete us or substitute a part of us we lack. Those holes we have won't be filled by other people, things, or places. They will fill us on the surface, but deep down those holes are still empty. It will be like putting a band aid on a cut you know you need stitches on. It will work at first, but eventually the wound will keep bleeding through the band aid, no matter how many we put on. The wound won't heal until we treat it properly. If we decide to keep replacing band aids (people and things), eventually the hole will feel closed. That is, until we remove the nasty scab that's been covering the surface of the wound. When we look for love and healing outside of ourselves our wounds won't be fully healed and we'll be left with a permanent scar inside.

Our energies don't complete each other; they are an equal exchange not a gap filler. In any healthy relationship there's no ownership,

51

completion, or dependency; there's partnership. We will have many types of relationships throughout life; friendships, family, and romance. But, we cannot depend on these relationships to fill us with the love we desire if we do not already possess it within ourselves. Our own self-love is infinite; it won't run out. However, many of these relationships can be seasonal lessons meaning they don't last forever; so we shouldn't use them to fill us up when they can easily leave us feeling empty again. Love from someone else does not and cannot replace the love we must find in ourselves.

The only type of love to fill those holes within ourselves the right way is self-love. Love is not searched for; it's already inside of us and it radiates to everyone around us. When our cup is constantly filled by our own self-love, we won't have to rely on people or things to fill us up. We won't have to live in fear we'll run out of what keeps us going. We will be unlimited and able to send out the highest energy of love. When we vibrate at a self-fulfilling high frequency we vibrate the same energy in everything we do. Then, the same energy will be attracted to us. New relationships will be formed, new opportunities will come knocking, and abundance can flow into our lives. The frequency of energy we have is the energy we attract. Love being the highest frequency.

Lack of Self-Love

A lack of self-love is an abundance of fear. When we see stories of people who commit the most hateful crimes, they are often dealing with the most painful tragedies. They can only show hurt to others because of how much fear and pain they have in themselves. Bullies; people who make it their mission to steal someone's happiness are often a bully to themselves or getting bullied by someone else. People who are suffering internally begin reflecting their own suffering to others. They feel so badly inside; they inflict that same pain to others because they want others to feel hurt like they feel hurt.

The opposite of love is fear; so when there is a lack of self-love within, many people are acting in fear. Fear brings out low vibrating qualities like pessimism and jealousy. Hailey the hater, whose always tryna talk shit on ya name? Well, when we look at her with compassion, we see Hailey probably hates something or everything about herself. Why would Hailey be concerned with anyone else's looks, image, possessions, and life if she truly loved her own? See, Hailey's self-worth and self-love comes from the opinions or people outside of her. So, when her amount of admiration and love from others is threatened by say iced out Iesha who just moved up the street. Fear kicks in and Hailey starts acting like she's been drinking haterade for the past 3 years because she needs her holes filled.

Haters are only people who see others shine and are attracted to it. They hate they feel so compelled by you and they see others are too. They hate they don't feel that way about themselves and others don't feel that way about them. All a lack of self-love. For Hailey and most haters, things out of their control have shaped these hating ass behaviors they project onto others. Our personalities are just ways we deal with our life trauma;

however, it's our responsibility to heal. When we have self-love, we know our own life is lit. Then, we don't compare; we congratulate.

Loving oneself based on the insecurities or trauma of others is also a lack of self-love. Many times we base on our self-image on the downfalls of our peers. We look at others and think, "well at least I'm not like them or have those issues", in order to build up our self-esteem. Women and men struggle with this. Women will look at other women and compare themselves. Sometimes we don't feel adequate, which causes behaviors similar to hatin Hailey, but sometimes we will feel as though we're superior. We will compare our body, the way we dress, our ability to pull men, and a million other things. Often, we will find one area where we feel we are better and use it to boost our self-esteem. With men, they will compare body count and other forms of quote of quote masculinity to boost their ego. I believe it's referred to as a pissing contest. Regardless, any form of building one's self-image based on comparing others to ourselves is a lack of self-love. Our self-image should have nothing to do with others. We shouldn't have to feel superior to be confident. We just have to love who we truly are.

Another common symptom of love deficiency is creating an unrealistic self to love. Many of us create a mask to show the outside world; this mask is who we desired to be, often due to societal standards, but not who we are. A mask can be hiding behind makeup, clothing, or portraying behavior which is not our own; which some may refer to as culture appropriation. Whatever the mask is, it's an inauthentic image portrayed to the outside world. Often to get others to love oneself and to create an ideal image for oneself to love. Newsflash, you can't love yourself if you only love the mask you put on. True self-love comes from loving every aspect of self in an open and authentic way.

Love Thyself

Our life is structured based on our self-image. Meaning, the perception we have of ourselves; who we are, our qualities, our worth, and all we believe we're capable of, is all we can attain in this life. It is directly correlated to the life we can live. Our own self-image is the image we project into this reality. For example, if we believe we are incredibly beautiful and capable of reaching extreme success, we will walk through this life with beauty and success. It all starts with how much love and confidence we have in ourselves. The love we have for ourselves determines the quality of life we experience, since the universe only responds to vibrations within self.

We often get trapped in this idea we will love ourselves when our situation gets better, when we get happier, and when we are more beautiful. It's the exact opposite. When we love ourselves, we become more beautiful, joyful, and attract better outcomes in life.

Lit Lena; she loves herself and everyone follows. Lit Lena focuses on her own reality, vibrates good energy, manifest her own dream life, and walks beautifully and confidently while doing it. When we love ourselves fully, everyone does too. Remember I said earlier, everyone is drawn to love and light. **When we vibrate high** we give off a magnetic energy; we have a Jen ne sais quoi about us which makes others feel the way we already feel about ourselves. People can only love us as deeply as we love ourselves and vice versa. Love is the highest frequency. When we carry such a high vibration within us, it's inevitable we will attract things, people, environments, and opportunities of the highest frequency possible. Love yourself and you will transfer love to others, attract love from others, attract a life of love and light, and make the universe brighter tonight. **#Naturalisthewaytoglow**

It's always there. Life does not exist without love; we do not exist without love. Love is light, abundance, joy, patience, forgiveness, compassion, and with no conditions. It's our natural state. The essence of life is unconditional love and we must first find it within ourselves. Dig deep, look within, and find love within yourself.

Activity

I Love Me

- Write down 20 things you love about yourself on sticky notes and place them on your mirrors, in your room, and in your bathroom. Remind yourself daily how lovely you are!

Chapter 3
Love for Others

Give Love

In High school we learned the Greek philosophy of love and how there are different forms of love energy. Although they have changed a bit, I still believe in this philosophy today. We already discussed the universal love which created us and already fills us. That unconditional love is referred to as Agape; an infinite Godly love. Then, there is the love we feel for others. Eros; which is erotic and romantic love. Felt in the physical body and associated with intimacy and sexual interaction. Storge; which is family and community love. Displayed through duty and loyalty . Lastly, Phileo; brotherly love or love we feel in close friendships.

Agape is the love we all have in us; the love of God universe, the love which creates life and holds it together. This love has infinite power over all and is not subject to human error. Eros, Storge, and Phileo are forms of love mixed with human energy; love that isn't always unconditional.

What You Give You Shall Receive

When I first studied the whole give and receive idea. I was still searching for love from outside of myself. So, I went around doing extremely kind things for people; going out of my way to make others feel loved. The thing is, I was doing this so the love I gave out would be returned right back to me; making me feel loved. I found myself suffering because of how much I did for everyone else and didn't get anything I was looking for back. When we give love we can't always expect it back how we want it. We can't assume because I did this for you, you owe me something. Although this was me giving out love; it surely wasn't unconditional. If the kindness wasn't shown back to me; I no longer wanted to give it. Unconditional love is loving no matter the circumstances. The thing about love is, we can't give out the genuine and unconditional kind if we don't have it within ourselves first. We also can't receive the genuine and unconditional kind unless we have it in us; for us.

"Pure love is a willingness to give without a thought of receiving anything in return."

-My Fortune Cookie

When we are connected to the universe, which is unconditional love, we have Agape source love to give to others as Eros, Storge, and Phileo. Agape is our base love and we must build Eros, Storge, and Phileo off of it.

Equal Love Exchange

Unconditional love for self means unconditional love for others. The most fulfilling sharing of love is when there is an infinite flow of love coming from within each whole being so each person can pour love into the other without drought. An equal exchange of unconditional love energy. I water you; you water me. Although this type of partnership is fulfilling, we don't depend on them to fill us up with love within; it's something we possess beforehand. It's like a cherry on top, instead of filling in holes for a lack of self-love, this love just adds on to our own. These relationships are special and a huge blessing in our lives. However, we'll come to find out, many people don't have the love from within required to pour out for equal energy exchange.

Loving Those with Less Love

When we find ourselves acquiring unconditional self-love we'll notice there may be people in our lives who have love within, but not as potent as we do. We can only receive and give love as deeply as we love ourselves. Meaning, people may not feel as deeply others. People may not be able to handle the depth of another person's love because they don't love themselves equally as deep. So, it becomes too consuming. Ever felt like you literally loved someone to death? Like your love for them was the same thing that pushed them away? Others can only receive love as deeply as they love themselves. I had to learn this lesson as well.

A friend of mine I met in college helped me go through a really tough time; he was truly a friend to me and I to him. The entire buildup of our friendship was the start of me truly beginning to love myself unconditionally. We both loved each other but the love I had in myself began to go deeper and deeper. Simultaneously the love I had for him did as well. I couldn't help but blurt it out in every way I could because I was beginning to overflow with love within. This very thing is what drove us apart; he felt consumed. My love became extremely deep, I learned to begin loving myself on a physical, mental, emotional, and spiritual level. I began falling in love with myself unconditionally; this makes my love for others just as deep. This type of love can be overwhelming and all-consuming to those accustomed to shallow waters. My LOVE, my soul, and my entire essence became deep like the ocean; others will swim or they will drown. I had to be okay with that. I couldn't be upset about him not loving me back the way I loved him because he didn't even have that type of love in himself to even give. The lesson didn't stop with just this one relationship; throughout my journey there have been several people I've had to detach from because they didn't match my capacity of love. So, they couldn't love me like I did them. Detach meaning still loving them with all my heart unconditionally just no longer allowing their actions (projections of love within themselves) affect me. Then I realized Truthfully this is how we should be with all people, things, and places. When we find ourselves full of unconditional love, part of it is accepting everyone can't love like we do. It has nothing to do with our value or worthiness of love; it's the other person's amount of self-love affecting their ability to love others.

The thing is, this form of love I gave was only Phileo; brotherly love. I can only imagine the power of my love in forms of Phileo, Storge, and Eros combined; the love I'll have for my life partner. I now welcome other deep sea divers willing to sail the ocean with me.

Loving Those Without Love

The opposite of love is fear. Those who lack love within are vibrating with fear; a low vibration. This isn't necessarily a negative thing; we shouldn't look down upon those vibrating low. Some part of their life has caused them to develop fear and survival tactics. Remember, I mentioned earlier, each person's personality is only a set of behaviors used to cope with personal life trauma. Ever had one of those teachers on some freedom writers type shit? Or been to a 8th grade/senior class retreat where everyone cries and spills out the shit they are going through? It's those moments that shows us, everyone has something going on. Think back on them when you ask why people are so fucked up; fearful, angry, depressed, and hateful. It's because those plus more problems still exist and only get heavier as we get older. Anything hurtful, fake, shady, or racist thing anyone does is rooted from fear within the self. Nothing others do is ever personal.

Some people are like weeds, still beautiful though they feed off of other plants and sometimes kill them. They were meant to grow there, Mother Nature placed them. We have to appreciate them for their purpose, uniqueness, and the part they place in our growth (pause: have y'all ever looked at weeds up close? The shape, the cut, and some even produce beautiful flowers) but also remove them from using up our energy of light.

We cannot judge others fall falling victim to the vibration of fear or temptation because we are not completely free from the same things. We are all human, all spirits on an earthy journey. We are in a place full of light but also evil, darkness, and low vibrations everywhere around us. We are all facing trials, obstacles, and temptations which are meant to be present in our lives. It it for us to learn to push past these, to learn from our mistakes and from others. Not to judge or looked down upon; but to learn from, understand, and have compassion for the same temptations which can drag our asses too. Also, understand everyone was raised differently, our actions and views toward life are different because our perspective is shaped by our own experience. Which for many is a very tough one; an experience based on survival. With that being said, learn to accept people where they are at. People are out here drowning in fear; it's causing us to hurt each other when all anyone really desires is love. Be love; to yourself and others.

There may be people we want to love but don't want to become too sucked into their issues. When we choose to love those without love we have power over the energy exchange. If their energy is vibration much lower than ours and we can feel the lack; we can protect our energy from receiving their low vibrations. We can ask for a barrier of protection from our angels, ancestors, and guides when we are around those low energies

64

(if you get jiggy with that). We can also simply be aware of our own energy; constantly checking what emotions, thoughts, and sensations we are feeling; especially after we leave from being around them. Life is balance, we can't be afraid to be around low vibrating energy. We must have control over ours and practice self-love daily. Then, there's also this beautiful thing called love from a distance. We can love someone unconditionally with everything inside of us, but still distance ourselves and detach.

Give love; receive love. Love is healing. While the other people are on their journey of finding love we can pour some of our loving energy into them to help them along the way. Often, that's all we can do. Believe me, those loving vibrations affect them in more ways they'll even admit; energy is powerful. So tell people the things that make them great, it could be someone's saving.

Although some would say not to pour our love into a cup with holes in it. I say there is a thin line between giving some of our love and giving too much. Yes, there are some people who we feel don't deserve our love at all. But, there are some who need it. The reality of it is, some people may not have what we have to give. Having a true sense of love from within is rare. So, when we do have this real type of love within us we shouldn't be selfish with our energy; just responsible. It's our choice and specific to our personal life who we give our love to and how much we give. We just have to remember to be aware of our own energy levels and not overextend ourselves. Remembering to replenish the love within us daily and put our self-love first; always. The most important relationship is the one we have with our self.

Love Languages

Now that we've covered giving out love; let's discuss how to. For those we choose to pour into from our vessel, there's ways to make it received to the max. In his book, *The Five Love Languages,* Gary Chapman shares *5 different ways of loving*; words of affirmation, physical touch, quality time, acts of service, and gifts.[3] These count for not only how we show Eros love but Storge and Phileo love as well. Everyone has a love language. Love languages are often known as the way a person receives love. However, I believe it is the language of how we receive love from others, how we give love to others, and how we show love to ourselves.

Words of Affirmation	Giving or receiving loving words vocally and even written. "I want you to know I love you."
Physical Touch	Giving or receiving touch such as hugs, kisses, and massages. "Can I have a hug?"
Quality Time	Spending time with and being in the present moment with another. "Let's watch a movie together just me and you."
Acts of Service	Going out of your way to offer or receive an act of service by/for another person. "I planned us a trip; I know your busy and need a break."
Gifts	Giving or receiving gifts. "I bought you a special gift."

How We Give Love to Others

Often times the way we give out our love the best is different from how we receive. Not always; the way we give and receive love could be the same. Personally, mine differ a bit. My giving love language is mostly physical touch with a small sliver of words of affirmation. When I have these moments where I realize, "wow I really love you" I get an overwhelming drive to touch the person. This might seem super sensual and it can be but it's usually not even what's on my mind. It's more of a desire to energetically transfer my love through the touch sense. It can come off as a hug, hand hold, a stroking of skin, or any contact that ignites the touch senses. However, because touch is automatically viewed as some sort of sexual connotation I often hold it back to avoid misunderstanding. Nevertheless, those who are aware of the way I show my love know how touchy feely I can be. Our giving love language is whatever we automatically desire to do or say for someone when we are in a state of love. If you feel a drive to tell someone you love them, yours may be words of affirmation. If you want to go out and get the most personal and special gift for someone, yours may be gift giving. We should know our giving love language, but also cater to others receiving love language in the way we give our love. Knowing someone's love language doesn't mean we should only show them love in that language; it's about being aware of how they feel loved the most.

How We Receive Love from Others

The only time I feel love energy through physical touch is when I have the drive to show love in the moment. For example, if I get a desire to hug someone and I begin to lean in for a hug, I will receive love back from the person by them also leaning in for a hug. There we both engage in physical contact leaving me and the other person (if that's their love language) feeling loved. However, when I am not in the mood to transfer my energy; it's safe for everyone not to touch me at all. Touch is not received unless I'm already in the mood for giving; it comes off as aggravating otherwise.

My true receiving love language is words of affirmation. It doesn't matter the time, place, or what mood I'm in, words will always make me feel loved. Simple words or detailed words it doesn't matter; the energy words carry are received so deeply within my spirit. If someone says, "wow you are a beautiful soul" this one sentence can leave me feeling so incredibly loved for days. As opposed to if someone bought me a gift. Though very much appreciated; it doesn't absorb like the energy of words do. Because of my receiving love language, my relationship with music is magical. When listening to songs with depth, I can become electrified by the lyrics. Good music gives me goosebumps. Our receiving love language is the energy we absorb in the deepest parts of us; the energy that stays with us mind, body, emotions, and spirit. It's whatever someone says or does leaving us with a magical energy flowing. Remember, there can always be more than one.

How We Show Love to Ourselves

When people speak of love languages it's usually not connected with how we can show love to ourselves the best; however, I think it aligns. For a long time, I believed my receiving love language was something I could only receive from others. I would fantasize about how amazing it would be if someone would just write me a hand written letter, sing to me, have a deep conversation, or spill out how much I mean to them. I would think about how much love I would feel within myself. As I began my self-love journey and realized love was already in me, I realized this magical feeling I get from words of affirmation did not have to come from outside of me. I didn't have to wait for some to write me a letter. Diving deeper into the unconditional love within myself made me look at love languages in a different perspective. Our love language is also, and in my opinion most importantly, how we show love to ourselves. Once I became conscious of this it made so much sense why affirmations motivate me so much. Words of affirmation is my love language; the words I speak to myself first and then words I hear from others. I can experience the same magical flow of energy within myself with my own words. This astonishing revelation lead to writing letters to myself about how amazing I am and how far I've come. I now have a collection of letters I read from me to me specific to whatever mood I'm in. I now listen to my own voice repeating affirmations about how incredible I am. I verbally tell myself daily how beautiful and loving I am. All of these words cultivate a magical love energy within my being at all times; without the need of anything or anyone outside of me. Never ceasing to cheer me up. If your receiving love language is physical touch, try getting to know your body. If yours is quality time, make time to spend with yourself daily; watching a movie, taking a bath, or whatever you prefer doing. If yours is gifts, treat yourself. Acts a service; stop procrastinating and do the dishes now rather than later, you'll feel much better. Better yet, do all of these things. Fill yourself up with every love language to create a life of love from within.

Part 2: Live Love

We've talked about the essence of love, the importance of our self-love, and giving love. Yet, everything keeps coming back to love from within. Let's dive a little deeper and get a little more personal. How do we truly create a life of love within for a life never without.

Chapter 4

Opening the Puzzle Box

Piecing the Puzzle

Have you ever started a puzzle, dumped out all the little pieces, and literally thought, "yo wtf?" How are all these little pieces going to come together? What type of picture is this going to make? You look at each piece trying to foretell the look of the finished product but everything is scattered. Each piece isn't enough to see everything for what it is. So, you slowly start matching pieces together. Some look really funky and some look really aesthetically pleasing. Some pieces even look like they don't belong to the puzzle. It takes time, reflection, and dedication until you start to see a glimpse of the end result. The question is, will you stop piecing the puzzle together because it doesn't make sense right now? Or, because it's going to take a lot of time and concentration? Will you leave the pieces scattered and disconnected? Are you satisfied being left curious to where every piece even went? Or will you use the bigger picture as your motivator? Knowing no matter how long it takes, how many retries, and confusing puzzle pieces that may come up, in the end something beautiful will come out of it.

"If you took all of your DNA and straightened it out, and put it end-to-end, it would stretch to Jupiter and back ten times over. You are neither small nor insignificant. Your just very well folded."

-Unknown

Our Puzzle Pieces

Aren't we lucky the exact puzzle pieces needed to make the picture already come with the box as a whole? We don't have to go searching through different boxes to find random pieces that may or may not fit together. Thanks to the puzzle constructor, who is the creator of the bigger picture, the box we have has every piece already included. This brings so much less stress knowing everything has already been planned, we don't have to control everything, we just have to align the pieces.

Metaphors are so lit because they truly connect to real life. God has already created our puzzle box, along with a little bit of our two cents. We have been given every piece we need. Opening other boxes to see if those pieces fit with ours is completely pointless. Ever catch yourself looking at someone else's life thinking "how do they do that?" or "I wish I could have that." Understand, It's because you weren't meant to; those puzzle piece didn't come in your box. We can't judge or be concerned with others paths because that is exactly the puzzle piece they need in their life to make the whole thing fit together. Their puzzle piece may be one you have never seen before, that doesn't fit in with, or look similar to yours. There may pieces from other boxes that look real nice and seemingly better than ours.

It's not about comparing boxes; life is not a competition. If it's not supposed to be, it's not in your box. It doesn't make your box any more or less valuable or of a beautiful picture, it makes your box unique. Every puzzle is different; some are one way and some another. The amazing thing about it is, our finished puzzle is perfectly designed for us.

Every single person was raised in the exact way, by the exact people, and in the exact place they needed in order to play the role they are supposed to in this life. Every single detail down to the core of our very existence has been magically placed like a puzzle. Every person, place, and thing has its place in our lives; they fit there because they are a piece to the bigger picture. Sometimes we don't understand why these pieces fit into or lives at this moment or the next. Some of these pieces may have brought more pain than anyone can understand. We have to love them anyway. In order to truly love who we are, we cannot hate or disregard the experiences which have shaped our lives. The circumstances we have encountered in our lives do not define us but they do tell the story of how we must walk in our divine path. When the bigger picture starts to come together we will understand why each little piece had to have its exact place.

Enough with the analogies. I think everyone sees what I'm getting at here. Everyone has their own unique path. Our lives are full of various aspects, characteristics, experiences, people, and environments ultimately shaping us into who we came here on earth to be. When we start focusing on our own path is when things finally start to make sense. You'll begin to see how I pieced things together the more you read.

From the moment the universe expanded a trillion atoms bonded, organisms grew, people met, and events orchestrated so you could be exactly who you are. No mistake was made. We all have a different path; no box is the same. That's the beauty of it all. Learn to love yourself including everything you come with and you will be unstoppable. **#Naturalisthewaytoglow**

Activity

Puzzle Pieces

Our puzzle pieces represent our own gifts, talents, love languages, experiences, home, family, friends, job, and every detail in our own life. This will start to come together more later; but, for now let's start looking at your puzzle pieces.

- Write down your unique gifts, talents, features, and traits. Don't be afraid to write down the difficult things such as: pain, abandonment wounds, regrets, secrets, fears, and underlying emotions. Write everything down in as much detail as possible. If you want your puzzle to really make sense you could even include your natal chart placements and numerology numbers.

Example
- My name is...
- I live in...
- I work at...
- I have __ siblings...
- My family is...
- My friends are...
- My talents are...
- My love language is...
- My insecurities are...
- I deal with...
- My sun sign is...
- My moon sign is..

- My rising sign is...
- My life path number is...
- My childhood was...
- My home is...
- I feel...
- My healthy traits are...
- My toxic traits are...
- I am fearful of...
- I'm passionate about
- I regret...
- I understand...

Save this for later.

Chapter 5
Finding Purpose

Before Purpose

Have you ever felt you were just drifting? Finding yourself doing what's safe, comfortable, and guaranteed to get you through this life. That was me. If you would have asked me a year ago what my purpose was, I would laugh and say, "why you just get so serious? ".

The Purpose of Life on Earth

The sole reason we are all here is to experiences each and every phase of life that creates us into our one and only self. We must use those experiences to grow and create life tools to lead toward living in our purpose. To do this we must find ourselves; piece our puzzle together, understand our gifts and talents so we can further develop them. Then, pair those gifts with our deepest desires. Finally, use your gifts and passions to serve the world around you. Then, you've got **purpose**. When we know and understand our purpose in this life, we can direct all our energy toward it. When we direct positive energy and emotion toward our purpose, we manifest it into reality, and live a purposeful life.

"Your purpose in life is to find your purpose and give your whole heart and soul to it."

-Buddha | Monk

For a long time, I lived life without a purpose. Not that I wasn't looking for one; I was. I looked for a deeper meaning in everything; but, I couldn't' find the fire to light the rest of the way. Reason being, I looked everywhere besides inside myself. I tried to align myself with societal preconceived destinations. I considered what everyone else told me I should be and thought maybe it would lead me closer. Searching for purpose in the outer world gave me no real answers. After I danced in the silence and I asked myself several forms of **Who Am I?**, purpose finally made her presence known.

What am I Good at?

I've always found it difficult to pinpoint my gifts. Something I truly love doing and wouldn't mind doing the rest of my life. The thing is, I bounce back and forth between different things. In my opinion, the world makes it seem like you can only be truly gifted in one thing; like you have to fit in a specific niche. The truth is, we are all multifaceted beings and most of us have more than one gift. Personally, it's hard for me to list myself under one category. I like to explore and expand on every last one of my gifts. Why neglect any? Even if it's not as significant or popular as another; gifts are special and magical. They all serve a fraction of our bigger purpose on earth. If you received five gifts specially made for you on your birthday, are you only going to open the largest one and leave the other four unwrapped and unused? Hell nah, you're going to open all of them. The less obvious ones could hold the most meaning.

1. Creating

Art can be a life lesson, a pain, a high, a dream, a message, or any part of our genius created. Something that can be heard, seen, tasted, smelled, or felt beautifully. It's not always understood or agreed with; each person can develop a different perception. The best part is, whatever we create comes from our highest self. This is how we become in tune with the universe; creating. Everything in life we know it is a product of the universe creatively expressing itself. Everything is art, so when we match this energy we are more in tune.

"Art is man's nature; nature is God's art."

82

-Phillip James Bailey

When we create we are giving a vibration through sight, sound, touch, smell, or taste. Which is why things like making visual art, making music, making candles, gardens, and foods are all forms of creation. They are all gifts we've been blessed with to give back to the universe. What we give out always comes back to us; which means, create. Period. In whatever way you like. It comes in all shape and sizes; just tap in. Art is our own magic we get to share. We often get caught up thinking only some are gifted in creating. Only some people are artist, can draw, paint, or sing. I believe all of us have a connection to creative energy; we just have to find it in ourselves. What we create is inherently art; not considered art by societal standards of what art looks like. We are all born creators; we are creation manifested. So, express thyself.

Although I believe all life has a connection to creative energy, I do think some have an urge to tap in more than others. For as long as I can remember, I've loved creating. From drawings, to making jewelry, ceramics, even my own room décor. According to numerology, this attribute is derived from my soul urge number three; meaning my soul has an urge to come alive and express itself through creativity of all kinds. Growing up, I always wondered which one of these specific ways of creating was my true gift. One of the best revelations I've had is realizing the act of creating is my gift and I can do it in more than one form.

One way I use my creative genius is through **painting**. It's something about the brush strokes and hand motions that are so therapeutic. It lights a fire in my heart knowing I created something so something beautiful. Passionately exploring the furthest limits of my perception I bring into the physical world a message through lines, symbols, and colors. My paintings tell a visual story to myself and others. The special thing about artwork is everyone can see what they desire. My message in the painting can be seen in many different ways. Plus, they look good on walls. However, I can't see myself being a full time artist for a living because I find it hard to create something when limitations are introduced.

Another way I create is through **fashion**; mixing colors and pieces to create the perfect aesthetic. When I like my outfit I feel like I'm straight queening. By the way, true fashionistas aren't materialistic. We actually enjoy choosing our clothing of choice; having different options to mix and match. It's not for everyone else, it's for us; because it's self-expression. When I'm truly tapped into my spirit; my outfits express my inner creativity no matter who likes it or not. Free fashionistas dress how they desire; their own form of creation. The desire to broadcast it is very different from dressing for the crowd; it's the same as artist wanting their work in a museum, show, or published. It's self-expression. Free fashionistas dress how they desire; their own form of creation. The desire to broadcast our creation is the same as artist wanting their work in a museum, show, or published. We all deserve to share our gifts. But, I will say it is easy to get caught up in dressing for the crowd. I've been sucked into that before too. When I say dressing for the crowd, I mean wearing fits only for the approval and liking of others.

Then, there's **photography**. Whether it's capturing the moment or posing for the frame you can always find me near a camera lens. This doesn't make me vain; it simply means I enjoy the art of photography. A photo can freeze a moment of adventure, creativity, emotion, or any memorable feeling into physical form. I create the visual and the moment and freeze it for my eyes to revisit the creation and share with others. A photo is worth a thousand words; a unique message, and that's art. If you can relate, don't listen to the haters who won't let you take your selfies or pictures of your food in peace.

My creativity stems from several sources; I also enjoy **cooking**, listening to my ancestors to decide what ingredients will create the perfect flavor. **Dancing**, making artistic movements with my body. **Poetry** is my shit too and I also like to **sing**, even though people have told me my whole life I can't, I've always had an urge to. So, I don't resist it; I sing all the time. I like to call myself a multifaceted creative.

2. Communicating

I'm a Gemini moon which means I'm stimulated by communication. I'm a curious and versatile; I like to express what's going on in up there. Gemini is a sign which carries the desire for an exchange of information and ideas. I have a craving to understand the world around me and share what I've learned and observed.

Communicating is like an open gate to pour out all the knowledge and wisdom I've learned. Similar to being a sponge; I constantly soak up information (books, videos, articles, and experiences etc.). Eventually the sponge has to release the water. The ability to speak my truth and share my learned wisdom with others is an invigorating experience; it's a release. It can make someone who enjoys writing, teaching, or speaking go on for a lifetime. One sentence, word, chapter, or article can shift the direction of a person's entire life for generations to follow.

I used to ponder the idea of whether I was meant to be a teacher, a writer, or a speaker. When I realized I was good at all of these things, I saw they are all just forms of communicating ideas. I don't have to limit my communication to one channel; I can communicate ideas in all of these ways.

3. Leading and Inspiring

I'm an Aries sun and Leo rising; this is a fiery combo. People with these signs have magnetic energy and extreme charisma; we naturally capture the attention of many around us. Leo energy is very loud and bold; the lions of the jungle and the rays of the sun. Aries are the leaders of the zodiac; we are the rams, the initiators, the doers, and the starters. This is because Aries energy is what brings in the new spring season after winter; the fiery energy that births all the new fruits of the season. Which in my opinion makes me a great fit to pursue entrepreneurship, leading, and lifestyle influencing. Now, a lot of people make it seems as if you know you turn heads and have an effect on the energy of a room, you are arrogant or stuck up. But truly, there are some people who naturally have the energy of a leader. We all know those people who when they speak people listen; they have command and presence. It makes no one better than the other, it's simply the role we are meant to play. The sooner you realize your skills the better.

For me I have a desire to create my own dream life; I want to inspire others to create theirs. Aries and Leo are fire signs which means I'm very passionate in all that I do. I'm always looking to light the fire in others I feel in me.

What do I Love Doing?

86

After I unwrapped my gifts, I began searching inside me for what it is I absolutely love doing. Something that may not be a gift but more like a deep longing or desire.

"Let yourself be silently drawn by the strange pull of what you really love. It will not lead you astray."
- **Rumi | Poet , Theologian, Jurist**

1. Traveling

I've always been a traveler. Growing up, between me and my sisters cheer competitions and my parents career, we traveled around four times a year; within the states. I always deeply enjoyed all of those trips but it wasn't until I went abroad in college I found my truest desire. An opportunity to study abroad in two countries stood before me. It was days before deadlines; even though it seemed irrational I had this feeling I should be on that exact trip. So I went for it. This was a time I used my intuition and didn't even know yet; I didn't know the reason for the feeling but I followed it. I was exactly right; that trip ended up being the most incredible experience I had ever had. While I was immersed into a brand new culture and exploring new ways of life, I found an intense joy shining within me; a joy I never felt before. This was my spiritual energy showing me what it feels like to truly walk in my own authenticity of love. Here, I was as close to my highest self than ever before. When we act on our passions we align with our spirit. Our spiritual energy is fire; passion is a that fiery energy coming through. Whatever sparks love within you as bright as stars is your passion.

When I connected that deep fiery joy within me, with my passion for foreign travels, I found another puzzle piece within me. Because I was able to pinpoint this deep desire I studied it more and understood why it is I truly love traveling.

Each place is different, which is what makes them so unique. This connects with my gift of communication. In order to communicate something, we must learn something first. When traveling, I learn something new every day. I study and observe so much about what's new around me and find myself exploring everything in my atmosphere. I find thrill in seeking out new adventure. When I travel, I am in a constant state of unknown. This gives me adrenaline and pumps me up to seek and understand everything about the place I am. Usually by the time I gain familiarity, it's time to explore the next place. We all know what an adrenaline junkie is; I like to refer to myself as an adventure and knowledge junkie.

What Ways do I Enjoy Giving Back?

1. Energy Healing

"The wound is where the light enters you."

-Rumi | Poet, Theologian, Jurist

It is often our deepest pain which allows us to transform into who we're destined to be. Where there's pain, there's purpose; our traumas are a part of our puzzle too. All of that hurt we had to experience has reason behind what we can see sometimes. Pains makes us stronger; when we face our pain it allows us to grow and accumulate knowledge of how to heal. With that knowledge and understanding of healing from certain wounds, it is our responsibility to share what we've learned with those around us. Healing from our own pain is key to helping the world heal.

I grew up with a sick mom; I depended on doctors to provide healing when all they really wanted was more money. It was always one thing after the next; take this pill, get this surgery, now pay for this treatment. In the medical industry, many black women are ignored and written off as faking it. Even if they are taken seriously, they are often given false hopes. Made to believe in a treatment never meant heal them. In reality it's all a game; it's all about profit. How much money can we make off these people?

Witnessing a decline in my own mother with no knowledge of how to help, generated a constant state of worry and helplessness growing up. Creating major anxiety that carried on into my adult years. When your mother hurts, you hurt; we all come from our mother's womb, we are our mothers.

It took me a long time to recognize this pain and even longer to heal it. When I did begin the healing process, it inspired me to help not only my mother but anyone experiencing pain (physical, spiritual, mental, or emotional) to begin healing as well. Experiencing the effects of sickness turned me into a healer. This was how I wanted to give back to world, with energy healing. A true healer knows healing is more than just physical, it's mental, emotional, and spiritual. It all comes down to energy. We must heal the energy within all of our energy bodies; the makeup of us.

It wasn't until I experienced a very traumatic event in my life did I recognize how much healing power I unlocked by healing my own energy. During my summer teaching internship, I was required to complete a mental health, first aid, and CPR/AED training. Having that knowledge under my belt was a blessing; but, I thought the chances of me using most of it was slim. Boy was I wrong. Two weeks in, there was a massive car accident right in front of the school. At the time, my scholars were outside playing as I watch them from inside the building. Suddenly, I saw students and teachers take off as if something was wrong. Naturally, I followed I didn't know any details of what happened, I just ran to the scene and fell to my knees. Right in front of me lied a 14-year-old girl in the grass screaming, crying, full of fear, and pleading she was in so much pain she couldn't breathe. Chaos filled the scene; traffic piled up, I heard voices calling 911, and bystanders crowding around asking what happened. People prayed mercy on this child. There in this moment everything paused. Was a little girl going to die in my arms? What do I do? My heart started racing faster than ever, then suddenly everything was calm. I could hear nothing in the background, a sense of utter peace filled my entire being. I did what I knew how, I checked her pulse, and I checked for wounds. All I could see is was an indention on her belly. The force of the seatbelt on her abdomen caused some sort of internal injury. There was no wound for me to stop the bleeding and she didn't need CPR. She was breathing but her breathe was short; she was in shock, in excruciating pain, and she was scared. The only thing for me to do until the ambulance arrived was use my energy. I needed to exchange my peace with her fear. I held her hand, rubbed my fingers through her hair, and spoke to her with the calmest and comforting voice I had in me. I promised she would be okay. I stayed right by her side until her mother and the ambulance took over. By the time I left she was still hurt but no longer screaming or short of breath. She gained a sense of calmness for her journey to the hospital. Later, after all my adrenaline faded, I had the most intense anxiety attack I had in while. It was like I gave her my energy and I took hers.

This was when I realized how much our energy can heal others mentally, physically, emotionally, or spiritually. Whether it be the energy transmitted through our touch, our voice, our writing, our work, or just our presence. It's all healing.

When we open ourselves up for the purpose of helping others, we can change lives on an incredibly deep level. For me and my purpose I learned it's my vulnerability, openness, and expression of my deepest truths that trigger the healing in others. With that being said, healing has to be decided and done from within the person who needs it. We can't heal everyone, we can only plant seeds to inspire.

Live a Purposeful Life

I found my purpose by discovering many puzzle pieces within me and piecing them together; what I'm good at, what I love to do, and how I give back to the world. Your passion feeds your spirit, your purpose feeds the world. Purpose is the reason we take this journey; passion is the fire in us that lights the way. The whole reason we are here on this earth is to complete our purpose; God gave us passion to make it enjoyable.

Now, if someone were to ask me, what is my purpose on this earth, I would stand up straight and confidently say, my purpose is to **explore** new ways of understanding love and life through **traveling**, reflecting, and welcoming new lessons. Then, **communicate/express** what I have learned through various forms of **creation** to **heal** and **inspire** others in order to raise the vibration of this planet.

When acting in my own purpose I am helping others heal while continuing to love and heal myself. I'm allowed to grow and explore each and every one of my gifts. I'm allowed to feed my desires while feeding the world around me. I'm not limited to one thing, I can't be put into a box, and I am free. Free to speak my truth, express my creativity, travel to unknown places, and free to live a life I dream of. **#Naturalisthewaytoglow**

Know Thyself

The only way to find purpose is to truly find yourself first. The things which bring us the most spark and what we are drawn to the most are no coincidence; these connect and point us closer to our passion and purpose in this world. We love the things we love because they are a part of our whole puzzle. We've been given the gifts we have because we will need those tools to be successful. So, we have to get to know ourselves to f gure out what those things are.

I think our favorite colors have to do with characteristics we have; things our soul urges for, things we are gifted at, or love doing. Every color is a different vibration of light energy; everything is energy. There's a reason why our eyes are attracted to a certain frequency more than others. These color vibrations represent different chakras which hold different traits within us. My favorite color ever is blue; blue looks so magical and peaceful to me. The color vibration makes me feel good. This coordinates with my throat chakra which governs expression, it's extremely open and at times overactive; a lot of energy flows there. I love to express myself in so many ways; I'm in love with communicating my truth. I also have a love language of words of affirmation. My soul urge number is 3; the urge to express oneself in various creative ways. Remember, I'm also a Gemini moon; deep down I love communication and am good at it. See how much of the same vibration flows through my essence. Blue, expression, communication, throat chakra; our favorite colors can tell so much about us.

If you're like me and quick to run with ideas, you'll probably think you've found your purpose many different times. The excitement of beginning to uncover pieces of yourself feels like you've got things figured out. You'll think, "I love fashion so I'll be a fashion designer or I love painting so I'll be an artist"; I've said those exact words out loud. The thing is, we're so used to fitting into these generic titles we think this is how we must act in our purpose. But our purpose is something bigger; it's a creation, its art, it doesn't fit in one category, it's a huge puzzle full of tiny pieces within us we must put together. Think about how long it took Beyoncé to prepare for Coachella; there's intricate details which need to be put together for the whole show to be a success. Our purpose is the same; finding it takes times which is why we've been given an entire lifetime to figure it out and put it into action. It's take tremendous effort and organization to put all the pieces together of our gifts and passions and figure out how we want to give to the world. Be patient and put your heart and soul into finding yourself, then, overtime you will find your purpose.

Using my natal chart as pieces to the puzzle allow me to understand and find love for myself on a much deeper level than I thought before. It had a lot to do with me finding my true purpose on this earth. There were tips that led me to really look deep within myself and discover what it was I passionate about and good at. After all, every arrangement in the universe has intention, the stars have messages for us to uncover about ourselves. After developing my own thoughts and putting my own puzzle pieces together I came across a detailed Aries description that pretty much summed up everything I just explained. When I came across this description I was floored by how shockingly accurate it was, yet, also very confirming. The description completely aligned with exactly what I found my purpose to be. Since I knew I was on the right track toward truly fulfilling my destiny, my inner self-love grew even deeper. Hopefully this inspires you to dig deeper into your own puzzle pieces to find your life's purpose. If you have a hard time believing in astrology, it may be persuasive if I mention our Afrakan Ancestor are the ones who brought this great knowledge from the stars to us. Nothing in the universe is pointless; everything is a mirror, everything has purpose.

Believe in Thyself

Once we find our purpose in life we often get caught in this idea of the market being too concentrated in what we want to do, "too many people are already doing it, there's crazy competition, and it's too late to try an enter it now" or even the idea "I'll never be able to make a career out of this, this won't make me enough money". All bullshit. Ask yourself, "is this my god given talent and purpose on this earth?" If so, there's nothing that should stop you. If this is your true purpose you fit perfectly into the puzzle piece of the market you want in; there is a place especially made for you. If this is your purpose the world has been crafted for you to act in t. We are one collective energy split into billions of puzzle pieces; each one unique and very well needed in creating a new world based on love. The world won't change with one act it is the union of several actions which brings about true change. Even though we worry about who's ahead of us or winning, in all reality there's no such thing as competition. Everyone's way of enacting their purpose is completely different and personal; we are all different, so what we have found in ourselves and decided to give to the world is one of a kind. Everyone's timing is different and no one's purpose is the same. Plus, there's enough money and success for the entire planet to be wealthy; it's all energy. Cut out all the self-doubt and worry about someone else's puzzle box; to pursue your purpose you must believe in it and in yourself.

94

Activity

Who Am I?

Go back to the questions forms of "who am I". This time, make it about yourself. Taking a look at your personal astrology and numerology chart may help. Look back at your puzzle pieces from the last chapter to help answer these questions.

1. What are my gifts/what am I naturally good at?
2. What do I love to do? (What brings you joy just thinking about it? What do you do that makes you forget to check your phone? What do you do that brings an unexplainable amount of energy and joy? Remember, it can be more than one thing. Can't think of anything? Start trying things and ask your higher self to reveal what it is you truly love. This can take time; have patience with yourself.)
3. What pain have I experienced and healed/need healing from?
4. What are some ways I can use these things to serve the world around me? (Think big; not surface level.)
5. What's my purpose? (Take your time finding this answer)

Chapter 6
Present on Purpose

When Does my Purpose Start?

Once we find our purpose, many of us have this idea we can't live it out until it is all here; when the whole business is set up, we have clients, our book is written, or when whatever big plans we have to live out our purpose is all here. Trust me, I've been through this mind trap before. The truth is, our purpose is right now; we can live in purpose anywhere, anytime, and with everything we have at this present moment.

I used to be so anxious about when I was going to be able to make my big moves and when my business was going to explode. So then, I could finally start acting in my purpose. Thankfully, I realized my purpose can be acted on in so many ways I'm missing out on. One day, I was shopping in the mall with my mom and I felt so present; I was paying attention to every detail surrounding me and every person I came across. I was really just living in the moment. We proceeded to go to Starbucks and I ordered my classic Matcha Green Tea Latte. While ordering, I noticed the cashier seemed extremely irritable, with no interest in taking my order. Now, old me would've caught an attitude and given them a stank look like, "yo you need to work on your customer service bro, it ain't my fault you here"; But, this time I was in the moment. I thought about how this person has an entire story I know nothing about. They could have kids who aren't doing well, parents who may have passed, they could have just stubbed their pinky toe, or dented the front of their car; little things. All of these possibilities rushed through my mind as I proceeded to order my latte. I decided to smile and intentionally shared some of my high vibrational energy. I greeted them with curiosity of how they were doing and wished them a great rest of their day. Instead of being in my own head and worrying about my life, my problems, and how fast or accurate someone is doing something for me, I opened my eyes and sat in the moment. Open to all possibilities. That's when I understood I can always act out my purpose; anywhere, any time.

Being present in the moment and shifting our awareness toward living in our purpose will always lead us to walking in line with our highest self. We'll always be able to seek out opportunities to further use our purpose in various ways. My purpose is energy healing; I can energy heal with my writing, my touch, my voice, and even with my presence alone. I don't have to wait on all my business plans to blow up, for me to travel, or create tons of art to act in my purpose. Though those things are still a part of the bigger picture, they will manifest in due timing. As for where I am now, there's still purpose for me. Because I was present this one time, I was able to see an opportunity to act in my purpose and greet the Starbucks cashier with kindness and compassion. Life is about realizing we are and always have been exactly where we need to be. There are ways we can implement purpose everywhere we go because we are there for a purpose; we just have to learn to stay present.

Staying Present

I always thought being very futuristic was an extremely good quality of mine. I still love this about myself, but it took a lesson for me to realize I can't always be looking past the present moment. During a super quiet and eventless time period of my life, I kept being accompanied by an inner restlessness. One day, I came across a quote on Instagram that mentioned, an inner restlessness or bored sensation is often a signal for a need to do some deep introspection. So, I opened myself up for some self-reflection. Randomly while sitting on my bed I started thinking about childhood coping mechanisms I've formed. I realized I always had to have something to look forward to. This is something I've been doing ever since I was a kid. I would be fueled by whatever cool thing I had to look forward to in the future. It could've been small things like going out to eat, hanging out with a friend, speaking to someone, or getting to wear a new fit. It could've been big things like traveling or an event. Whatever it was, I looked toward it to get me excited in the moment. I always looked at what was ahead of me just to keep me going. Upon further evaluation I realize this was a coping mechanism for anxiety.

"If you are depressed, you are living in the past. If you are anxious, you are living in the future. If you are at peace, you are living in the present."
-Tao Tzu | Chinese Philosopher

Whenever I would have a moment of anxiety or inner restlessness inside I would flip the script and turn it into something I could look forward to instead of fear. Doing this helped calm me down immediately, it would switch my brain from fear to excitement or enjoying whatever I had ahead of me. But, I never looked at what I had right in front of me. Or, the deeper reason behind why I was feeling anxious in the first place. Whatever I thought of in the future could've been an hour away, a day, a week, or even a month. Regardless, it was always something ahead of me. I then understood this was something I carried into adulthood. When I'm feeling anxious I always search for something to look forward to and take my mind off what's currently going on inside of me; this alleviates my anxiety. When really I'm still living in the future causing more of it. That quiet and eventless time period of my life helped me uncover this coping style, I had nothing to look forward to when I felt anxious in the moment. So, I was forced to figure out why I felt that way instead of distracting myself.

After this revelation, I realize I truly needed to learn how to be in the present more often than not. I made myself a promise anytime I would have a restless or an anxious feeling I would stay present; asking myself what it is right here in this moment that's making me feel this way (usually me subconsciously fearing the future). Sometimes I figure it out right away, but if I don't I then go on to count my blessings in the moment. I stop and think about all the love within me and all the blessings surrounding me right here, which always brings me to state of peace.

Present Creates Reality

Our present vibration is what creates our reality. Because my present vibration was constantly looking forward to something better than what I was experiencing, it was holding me back from manifesting my desired reality. I created a constant flow of looking ahead; looking forward to the next best thing instead of enjoying what I had right here. So, I wasn't attracting more abundance to me in the moment I was constantly striving for something in front of me that would never come. Unless, I finally realize all that I had right here, right now. There's never a day exactly the same; every single day is a unique day. We have to look around and observe all things; look for ways we can fulfill our purpose wherever we are in the moment, look for things to be grateful for in the moment, and we will manifest more of these things in our future. You won't be able to manifest your desired reality by only wishing yourself out of the one your experiencing

Awareness

"Where awareness flows energy goes."
-Dandipani | Hindu Priest, International Speaker

Whatever we are thinking about in the moment or being aware of is where our energy is flowing. Whatever energy is constantly flowing is attracting more of that energy. For example, if you are in a constant state of gratitude you are attracting more energy of gratitude. You are attracting more things to be grateful for.

Story time; once upon a night I was showering super late around 2 am. Suddenly, I started feeling like I was in danger, like somebody or something was going to jump out and get me. Everything kept scaring me; the creek of the door to the sound of the wind. We've all had those moments. Anyway, I thought to myself, I'm only scared because my awareness is in the area of my brain which processes fear. So, I decided to change my awareness. I started thinking about all the things I was grateful for in my life. Then, before I knew it I was out of the shower; no longer in fear of what might have jumped out.

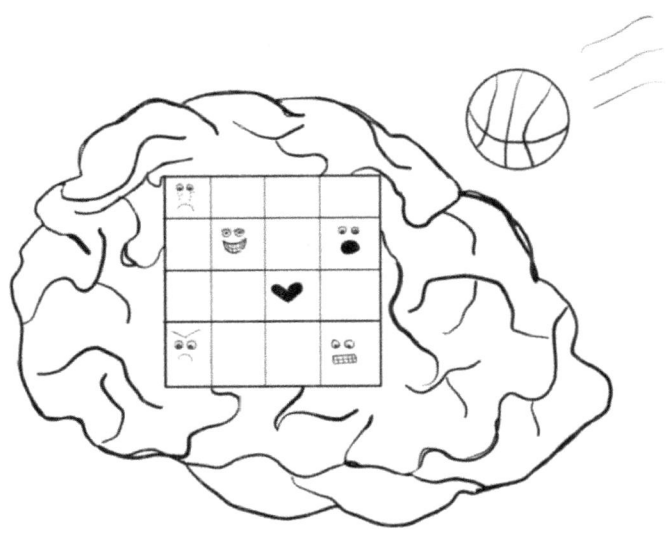

We have a mind full of compartments; these compartments can process hunger, boredom, sadness, anger, joy, or excitement etc. Think of our awareness as a basketball we can shoot into one of those hoops. If we toss our awareness into the hunger compartment, we will think about how hungry we are and begin feeling hunger pangs. If we take our awareness out of our hunger compartment and shoot it into our happiness one, we'll begin to feel happy. They key is to have control over which compartment our awareness is in.

The cool thing is, whenever we take our awareness from a low vibrational thought like fear and shoot it into a high vibrating one like joy, we weaken those the neurological pathways those old self depreciating thoughts traveled through and strengthen the new one we switched to. By switching my awareness from fear to gratitude I weakened my brain patterns which produced fear and strengthened the ones that produced gratitude. The more we do this the more we can debilitate our negative thought patterns and attract energy flowing at a higher vibration. Be the ball player of your own awareness. Don't just shoot the ball of awareness, dunk that shit into gratitude and purpose as much as you can; then, yell "AND ONE!". You will continue to flow in an energy of love and attract more to you.

However, we can't always operate in a joyful energy; sometimes we have to feel. Sometimes our brain has lead us to these compartments for a reason; to show us something...

Activity 1

Presence

- Make a mental list of all you have to be grateful for here and now.

- Repeat daily and again when you catch yourself swimming around in fearful thoughts of the past or future.

Activity 2

Make a playlist

- Let it play without changing any song. Be present enough not to control what's in the now. Allow yourself to feel each mood, open your mind, hear each prospective without judgment. Trust the vibe. Let the playlist take you on a roller coaster of various emotions, moods, and perspectives of life. Surrender, be one with the music, learn to breathe with it, get in rhythm, and flow.

- Do this while staying still, driving, and working out.

- Apply this concept to the music of everyday life.

Chapter 7 Emotional Energy

Here we are, back to the topic I promised I'd discuss in depth.

Why You in Your Feelings?

Everybody is always talking about "man get out your feelings!" or "why you in your feels?".
How about the question, "why you trying to avoid your feelings?"

All of us get emotional; it's a part of the human experience. Sadness, anxiety, guilt, happiness, excitement, anger, shame, jealously, or whatever. We love to really feel the good stuff; we even boast about it to our friends. But, what about the emotions that don't feel good?

Remember we talked about how our physical, mental, emotional, and spiritual body connect with the four elements of life; earth, air, water, and fire. These elements are also associated with astrological signs. Our astrology can tell us a lot about why we act the way we do and things we struggle with. It's easier for me to connect with my spiritual side because I have so many fire signs in my full astrology chart; fire is spiritual. However, the water signs in my entire chart hold a small percentage. Although I am still extremely emotional as a female, it's harder for me to let it flow; I really have to dig deep down. All things pertaining astrology can be confusing just glancing at it. I encourage adding your complete astrology chart to your puzzle pieces from earlier to better understand yourself. It's your choice; but, back to emotional energy. I've come to the realization I avoid feeling my emotions at all cost; at least the ones that don't feel so good. I suppress the not so good feelings I get on daily basis. When I say suppress I mean a variety of things. Suppressing by putting to the side, ignoring, or distracting myself from the experience. A lack of flow.

Examples

1. Let's say a friend does something really hurtful to me. I may sit there and shed a tear or two (max). Then, I'll quickly go into denial. I'll tell myself I don't care or that bitch was fake anyway. Then, proceed to roll up and eat some good food, "Ah, I'm better now; I should have never tripped in the first place".

2. Let's say my sister says something to me that really pisses me off. My brain starts processing anger; my energy starts flowing in anger. I may sit there and replay the scenario in my head a couple times (max). Then, proceed with distracting myself. I'll get on Instagram or YouTube and scroll for hours until I've calmed down and forgotten why I was mad in the first place.

3. Let's say I'm feeling insecure about something. My environment, my situation, job, physical appearance, or anything really. My brain tells me damn I'm sad; my energy starts flowing in sadness because that's how I'm feeling. I may sit there and wallow in my sadness for a few minutes (max). Then, proceed to put the sadness to the side. I'll call a friend; usually a loud and upbeat person and talk to them for hours. I won't mention to them two minutes ago I was feeling sad; I'll just carry on a casual conversation so I forget.

We're The Same

Whether you realize it or not, most of us are the same; one way or another. You might go workout for hours, go out and get drunk with friends, pop some pills, or catch another body. We all don't want to feel low vibrational emotions; we bury them and distract ourselves with something more pleasing. We can't beat ourselves up about it though. Majority of us, especially in the black community weren't taught how to feel our emotions. We've been given this idea of crying being a weakness; even more for men. Growing up we're told "you betta stop all that cryin before I give you sum to cry about!", so we've learned to suck that shit right back up and hold it in. This cultural idea of emotional weakness has caused many of us to bottle everything up inside; we chose to ignore emotion which is present in us. The thing is, enclosing our feelings without letting them be free flowing is emotional enslavement. But, we can grow from this.

The Problem

See the problem with these scenarios of putting to the side, distracting, and ignoring emotions is we think the feelings are no longer there. But, really we've just suppressed them, buried them, and pushed them deep down. All the while we're just playing ourselves; they're not gone. One thing about energy is, it never ends. Low vibrational energy stays low until we change it to high vibrating energy. We attract the energy we carry. If we keep burying and suppressing our emotions they will sit, attract more of the same energy, and begin to take a toll on us mentally and physically.

"We cannot overcome what we ignore."

Vanessa Van Edwards | Behavioral investigator, Author

Emotions Growing Stronger

Let's go back to the examples of how I suppress my feelings. All those energies from my emotions were still floating around in my energetic field. The next day would come and I'd run into a different low emotion. Then, suppress it again. The more days that went by, the stronger the low energy in my energetic field got. If we keep adding unsolved feelings to the ignore it pile; those low vibrations will build up, getting stronger and stronger. Then, attract more. Someone would eat some of my food and I would cuss them the hell out. Then, later I'd asked myself, why am I so mad? What's wrong with me? Something wouldn't go my way and I'd burst into tears like my life was falling apart. Then, later asked myself, "why am I so sensitive?"

One Thousand Little Things

It wasn't one thing that sent me spiraling downhill, it was a thousand little things I had been carrying around. A thousand things day after day I suppressed. Emotions I thought I got rid of but I just ignored. I had been carrying around emotional baggage which was only weighing me down and lowering my vibration.

"We heel by releasing. We don't heal by suppressing."

-Unknown

Usually when we overreact or get upset about something small it's not actually the thing which upset us. It just triggered something deeper. Anything which triggers us is directing us toward what it is inside we need to heal. So, when we see ourselves cussing out one of our friends for backing out of plans, maybe we aren't really upset about not having them there, were being triggered. Our friend may have triggered something inside of us that hates unreliability. Maybe something happened in our childhood that proved someone to be extremely unreliable and we still haven't healed from it. We still have anger built up toward it because we buried it when we felt emotion. So, whenever someone shows themselves to be even a little bit unreliable we are triggered and we react. Pay attention to those things that trigger you and make some time for introspection. Dig deep to find out what's really the source of this emotion. What event or person do we have an unhealed wound from that we need to assess.

(E) motion

Emotion is literally energy in motion. When we feel a certain emotion it's our energy asking us to move our emotion through our body and release it. We covered high and low vibrations earlier; negative emotions are just low vibrations clinging to our energy. Everything is life, all vibrations are alive. I think of hard emotions as low vibrating spirits searching for light. All darkness is attracted to light; so those low vibrations cling to us like mosquitos. When we feel them; our energy is asking us to move them through us and release them in a higher vibration. When we suppress them; we keep them trapped in our energy field. If we let these low vibrating spirit stay in our energy they will make it their home and begin lowering the vibration of our entire essence. We will begin suffering emotionally. They will lower the vibration of our minds, leaving us with various types of mental illness. Then they will lower the vibration of our bodies making us suffer physically from sickness. Release these emotions which are meant to MOVE through us; not stay. We are energy; in order to keep our emotional energy body vibrating high we have to let our emotions flow. We have to feel, heal, and release them.

"If you haven't healed, every time you think about a negative event from your past, your body produces the exact same chemicals in the body as when it happened. That means you relive the experience hundreds of times simply because you haven't let it go."

- **Unknown**

We have to let past and present emotions flow and also open ourselves up to future ones. Know we will face many hard emotions because we can't avoid them. Water is just a part of life's elements. I realize many of us have this idea of not being caught up in our feels; catching flights not feelings, I get it. Before I understood the importance of emotions, I attempted removing them from the scenario. So no one or nothing had the power to get me in my feelings. Especially not these lil

112

boys and girls. I kept myself guarded at all times to avoid ever being hurt. Some would say I was distant or mean. I kept my inner child, my vulnerability, my emotions, and darkness all hidden. Which is why a lot of people don't know much about me. My emotional body was blocked off from everyone. I thought I was doing a good job protecting myself but I was only hurting myself by denying an element of my being. Moving through life trying to cut off my emotions almost made me cold. We are not meant to be robots operating on intellect; we are made to feel.

After several lessons, I realized it's okay to feel; to feel good and feel hurt. Regardless of whether we are feeling pain or pleasure we must welcome all emotions. Avoiding and holding in emotions blocks the sacral chakra; keeping natural energy from flowing. We just have to trust the universe and open ourselves up to truly feeling. Whether this leads to high or low moments, know all feelings are necessary to this life path. They are teachers and we must let them help us learn. When we experience an emotion running through us. It is presenting an opportunity for us to grow. Welcome it, feel it, and overcome it.

"This being human is a guest house.

Every morning a new arrival.

A joy, a depression, a meanness,

Some momentary awareness comes

As an unexpected visitor.

Welcome and entertain them all!

Even if they are a crowd of sorrows,

Who violently sweep your house

Empty of its furniture,

Still, treat each guest honorably.

He may be clearing you out

For some new delight.

The dark though, the shame, the malice,

Meet them at the door laughing,

And invite them in.

Be grateful for whoever comes,

Because each has been sent

As a guide from beyond"

Rumi | Poet, Theologian, Jurist

I've learned I have to feel my emotions; I have to sit in it. No matter how painful; sit in it. Put away my phone, put down the bag of chips, and don't try to escape but dive deep into self. Isolate myself, look within, and feel that shit. Sometimes I'll cry, sometimes I'll meditate, sometimes I'll journal, or write a poem. Sometimes I'll scream and hit a pillow. I've learned to honor my feelings instead of judging them because every single time, I learn something. I get to the deep rooted issue of why I felt that way in the first place. It's not about wallowing in our emotions or ignoring them. It's about feeling them while they are present, learning from them, and then releasing. Water is powerful just like our emotions; we can choose to let the waves crash in and drown us or let them carry us across the water and float. Don't resist; just let it flow.

"It's okay to lose your shit sometimes, because if you keep your shit, you end up full of shit. Then you'll explode and there'll be shit everywhere. It'll be a shit storm, and nobody wants that."

-Unknown

When we first hit the topic of emotional energy I mentioned it correlates with the element of water. Water is how we keep our emotional energy flowing. Our tears are made from water inside of us. Like most, I used to hold back by tears almost every time I got the urge to cry. This was because I associated it with making me look and feel weak. I've learned over time crying is huge release of emotional energy; crying is healing. Now, I look forward to crying, I enjoy getting everything out. Crying isn't always a release a low vibrational energy; we cry when we are happy too. It's us allowing whatever emotion, whether it be grief, anger, or happiness flow through us freely. Go cry.

Find a way to release by not only crying, but expressing those emotions. We have to express our emotions as a part of releasing them. Tell people how they made you feel; If you felt hurt or loved. Regardless of if it makes you feel vulnerable or not. No relationship of any form can grow without vulnerability and self-expression. Express yourself in your speech, music, dance, writing, drawing, cooking etc. allow yourself to release how you feel or you will be drowned. Water must be moved.

Water is also associated with creative energy and the sacral chakra. Meaning, the emotions flowing through us also present an opportunity for creative expression in many forms. Release your emotions and allow the darkness to transform to light. Leaving behind a transparent powerful work of art which can evoke inspiration and emotional healing in all those who experience it. When we are tapped into the oneness of the universe creation becomes so effortless. It flows through us like water. Movements, Visuals, lyrics, and every sort of creative way of expression can pour into our being when we surrender.

New Example

1. My dad says something to me that really gets under my skin; I mean really rubs me the wrong way. I get mad; my energy flows in anger. Instead of distracting myself, I sit in it. I don't fall victim to it, drown in it, and let myself cuss everyone out (at least I try not to). I sit in awareness of this anger; more like a realization of the emotion being present and letting it teach me. I allow this emotion to flow through me and I journal about how I'm feeling. Suddenly, maybe even an hour or day later, I realize the things that bother us the most about other people are really just reflections of ourselves (next chapter lesson).

So, because I allowed my emotion to flow with ease I was able to understand why this anger was triggered in me in the first place. I was able to learn from my guest and honor its presence because it helped me grow.

Alchemy

Every person in our lives is a teacher. Every situation and emotion we face, minor or extreme, is a teaching moment. Once we gain understanding, we can turn those low vibrating energies into something positive. That, my friends, is called alchemy. This is how we grow and evolve. I now look at every emotion I face and ask myself not "why is this happening to me?" but "what is this trying to teach me?". Then, how can I apply this lesson to my life to further my growth.

"These pains you feel are messengers. Listen to them."
Rumi | Poet, Theologian, Jurist
-

These emotions are not meant for us to avoid; they are meant for us to solve. We are all alchemists. Capable of turning darkness into light, pain into purpose, weakness into strength, and low vibrating energy into high vibrations. So, next time someone hit you with some bullshit like, 'Why you in your feelings?" Tell them you aren't interested in being a fake savage, you're meant to feel, heal, and grow. **#Naturalisthewaytoglow**

Activity 1

Freestyle

1. Go to a quiet place alone where you are free from judgment or worries.
2. Play an instrumental, fast pace, slow pace, or play an instrument yourself if you can.
3. Listen to how the music makes you feel; really feel every sound wave.
4. Let whatever emotion you associate with the sound begin to flow through you (an instrumental may remind you of victory, heartbreak, joy or anger).
5. Be your emotional energy body, imagine your body made of water, let the waves take over effortlessly.
6. Don't think, don't worry, don't try to resist or control. Just ride the wave.
7. Begin freestyling in whatever way you feel called to. (Dance, sing, rap, spoken word)

Activity 2

Emotional Release

1. **Ponder the following questions:** What emotions am I holding in? When is the last time I cried or wanted to cry but didn't let myself?
2. Allow what your feeling to come up and be present.
3. Picture your emotions as lost people or spirits of low vibration inside you.
4. When they come to you picture yourself seeing that emotion trying to take shelter inside you instead of letting it take over.
5. Ask the lost spirit to show you who they are. Whatever you are feeling emotionally is the spirit inside you.
6. Say sadness reveals herself to you; ask sadness why she is here? What is she trying to teach you?
7. Once you start understanding why she is inhabiting space in your energy. Ask her if she wants to be sad anymore?
8. Speak kind words to her; read her affirmations and reassure her that she can be more than sad. Tell her she is light and love.
9. Now take a deep breath, inhale and picture the air in your lungs surrounding sadness inside your gut like a hug. Once you have her bring her up to the top of your throat exhale and release sadness. Scream, cry, sing, rap, or do whatever you need to release sadness. Send her on her way (remember to send sadness as a high vibration and not a low one; low vibes will come back to you).
10. This process can be repeated as many times for as long as you need it to, be patient with yourself.

Chapter 8
Mirrors

Room Full of Mirrors

Like attracts like. Here we go again with this ever so revolving explanation for energies within our reality. Let's do some warm ups; remember how frequencies and vibrations work? The vibration you are and send out is the vibration you attract. We create a vibration of energy within and around us; vibrations having the same frequency cling together and attract those of similar frequencies. So, the vibration you are currently carrying and sending out is coming back to you in many other forms that match yours. Meaning everything around us is a mirror for our own vibrations.

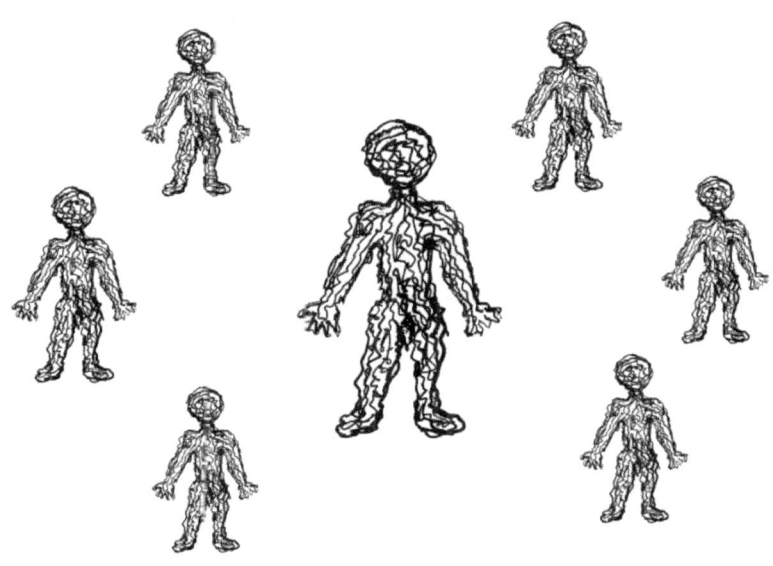

I find myself shook each time I sit back and think, everything in my life is a reflection of me. I'm looking at a part of myself that is vibrating high or vibrating low. The whole thing is a hard pill to swallow; it requires us to recognize and call ourselves out on our shit. Then, do the internal work to fix it. It takes deep self-reflection to turn the finger around and point it in our direction. When I decided to stop playing the blame game I recognized many faults and unhealed parts of myself.

Strangers

Not every single thing a mirror does is reflecting something within us; people do dumb shit all the time that has nothing to do with us. But it's the things in them we particularly react to, are fearful of, really admire, or are really bothered by. People who we see online or in public can also act as mirrors to us. If their particular lifestyle, the way they express, love, or carry themselves bothers us and makes us cringe full of judgment, we have met a mirror. Those judgments are keys to things we haven't healed within. Personally, I used to be so judgmental when I saw people post ass shaking videos or heard R rated songs about busting, riding, and slobbing. Then, after apply the mirror concept I realized I reacted so much because I hadn't healed the shame associated with freely expressing my own sexuality. Which is what a lot of us deal with since were taught sex equals sin. So, I judged; hard. It was easier to judge then to look at myself and understand why I couldn't do those things and express myself in that way without shame. After I began healing this within myself, I'd see the same videos, hear the same song, and be like aye fuck it up then. This was a reflection of my own healing.

Another example, there was a point in time where I felt like so many people around me were trying to impress me with intelligence. Specifically, males tryna holla at ya girl, since I often mention I'm sapiosexual; attracted to the brain. So, it was like every person trying to slide in the dms or build a relationship with me was trying desperately hard to strike a deep conversation or use twenty big words in one sentence. Acting like Tip. I could instantly tell when something wasn't flowing or coming off natural; I knew the energy of seeking to impress. I like authenticity from others; so, this bothered me. Because I was so open to acknowledging my flaws, I realized this is a mirror to my own behavior. If there was ever a time I wanted to impress someone, I always make it a point to exert my intelligence over my physical attraction because I have this thing where I'd much rather be loved for my brain than just my body. When the real gag is, I don't have to try to be loved for anything but just being myself. Whenever I would portray this behavior of stepping out of my normal character to impress it's like my spirit inside would be thinking, "bih, why you doing the most." Then, showed me how it feels when I do that; but, through other people. As annoyed as I was with the forceful intellect was as annoyed as my spirit was with my ego. My spiritual energy was begging for my own authenticity.

Friendships/Acquaintances

Anyone who is grabbing your attention or upsetting you on a serious level is a soul who is meant to teach you a lesson or identify something hidden in you which needs to be healed. Every soul we come across shows up as a mirror for something we need to work on; masked as things we dislike about that person. Also, the good qualities we have; masked as things we really love about that person. This realization helped me be present and look deeply into everything around me. My reality is a projection of myself. I studied people in my present and even in my past to truly see the proof of this phenomenon. As I reflected back on the memories of my past I saw so many mirrors of past pain I had not healed yet. I used to be the one who always complained about having the fakest friends ever. I found it easy to play the victim and only see what people were doing to me; always pointing the finger outward when I need to take a look at myself. The hardest thing was taking accountability for my side of the story; what did I do wrong in this relationship. When a friendship or acquaintance falls out, not fades away but falls out, both parties play a role.

When I looked at my past friendships as mirrors I realized all of us were suffering similar wounds and projecting them on one another. We were all mirrors to the unhealed parts of each other. Everything I felt they were doing to me, I created; I projected that negative energy in some form and it was only coming back to me. I was just too in denial to see those pains within myself.

"Your perception of me is a reflection of you; my reaction to you is an awareness of me."

-Unknown

Another fault of my own I realized is, I am extremely hard on other people; one wrong doing and your dead to me, easily. My cut off game is strong a hell; the gag is, cutting everyone off can be hella problematic. When I applied the mirror phenomenon I realized as hard as I am on others is as hard as I am on myself. I am my own biggest critic; I have this thing where I want to be perfect in every way. I Want to have perfect grades, perfect personality, perfect hair, perfect diet, perfect body etc. I push myself so hard to be the best at everything I do and when I mess up it's like

I cut off love for myself. I love myself so much for all of my good qualities; in fact, I often want to be good at everything so I can love myself more and quite honestly so others will love me more too. But the not so good qualities, I lack love for; I feel that because I have made a human error I am no longer worthy and this reflects in the way I treat others. I cannot truly love others for who they are until I learn to love all of myself; as a mirror, others cannot love my human faults until I do. I had to find a balance between cutting off people who are truly toxic and having patience for those who are simply human; just like me.

I met this woman in college who I admired so much; she was gorgeous, super intelligent, a fashionista, and had the kindest spirit. She was one of those people who you would never catch off her game; she stayed ten toes down. She ate healthy, worked out consistently, and her room was always clean; it seemed like she was perfect. She held herself up to such a high standard and I loved it. However, whenever I was around her I felt like I had to be perfect too; like I could not let my imperfect side show. Her energy was very intense; but my reaction to her energy had nothing to do with her, it was an awareness of me. Her spirit brought a lesson for me to learn. When I was in her presence, I felt like I was walking on eggshells. Not in a bad way, it was just because she held herself up so high I had to do the same. I could not make any human errors because it seemed like she never did. It took me a long time to realized she was a super mirror for me; I mean we had so much in common it was scary. We both strived for greatness in every aspect of our lives. The way I felt around her, was the same way I felt about myself deep down and how many others feel around me. Like we had to be perfect. Now that I was aware of this reflection, it made me want to continue carrying myself at a high standard; yet, learn how important it is to balance that standard. Not being so hard on myself, but hard enough. When I find this balance between accepting human error and bettering myself, this will reflect in my relationships. I won't expect others to be perfect and cut them off so easily; others around me won't feel like they have to be perfect. This way I will attract others just as committed to growth as I am, but at the same time we will all freely love ourselves and each other for who we are; which is imperfect.

Our mirrors are not only here to point out our areas of needed growth; but, also the areas we have grown and the parts of us that radiate light and love. When I see someone who I admire, who I think is strong, beautiful, or down to earth; I am seeing myself. My spirit is showing me a ray of light within me. I wouldn't see it if it did not exist in my own energy already. This realization has brought a great deal of appreciation in my life; when I look around at all the incredible people and things I fall in love with myself that much more.

Romantic Relationships

Another mirror aspect comes in with romantic relationships. The purpose of all relationships in our life is to be a mirror for healing and learning unconditional love. Our deepest wounds and imperfections rise to the surface when we are in relationships. Therefore, the deepest healing is done in partnership because the other(s) can expose the work needed, we may not see in ourselves. When you are in a relationship and you reach a conflict, know it's not you two (3,4,5 whatever) against each other; it is you two against the problem. The problem, more like a lesson, is present in each of you (often seeming present in one) to reflect back to one another; causing an emotion or reaction to surface. Which is there to be expressed, reflected on, felt, and released by all peers. Bringing more love into each person. Therefore, in partnerships we have an advantage of grow when we see these lessons as us two against the problem and work together and not against.

Our relationships are here to help us understand ourselves and learn to love on a deeper level than when we were alone. Deep soul relationships are ones where both agree to grow no matter what. Whether this relationship is with the opposite or same sex; whether it's with one other person or multiple. It's a commitment to heal past wounds that trigger each other and continue to grow stronger. It's about learning love and connection; what humans desire the most and what brings us to a high vibratory level. All relationships we experience are beautiful blessings we need to move forward in our life path. These triggers and misunderstandings that pop up are to be gifts and not obstacles toward healing together.

The ones who's love is felt on a deep level can only love this deeply because they love themselves. Those who love themselves on a mental, emotional, physical, and spiritual level can love others in that way. Their love can be felt in the bones and down to our very essence. We know like attracts like; so, that love for self will attract another being with self-love. The soul we attract loves itself as much as we love ourselves and loves as deeply as we love ourselves. We are vibrating in alignment with our relationships. Even what we love about people is a reflection of the things we love about ourselves. When we find ourselves in relationships where we don't feel loved unconditionally, it's because we don't love ourselves unconditionally quite yet. But that mirror is there to help us learn. Not all of romantic relationships are there to be forever, some only last seasons, and bring hard lessons we need in life. Regardless the relationship is always a mirror to how much we love ourselves in that season.

If you want attract true loving relationships; find yourself and love yourself first. Everything we desire most in a partner is everything we already are and things we desire to uncover within ourselves. Instead of using people outside of us to fulfill those longings, all we have to do is find it in ourselves. So, we have to unlock and find pieces of ourselves in order to align with our divine partner. We have to awaken each element of the person we want to attract, within ourselves first. Be the mirror. Example, if you want somebody who is fit, start going to the gym. If you want someone bilingual, start learning a new language. If you want someone who takes good care of themselves, take care of yourself. The only way to attract true love is by finding it within ourselves.

"You're not looking for love. You are looking for you. When you find and discover you, love will reveal itself."

-Unknown

Though we need to love ourselves before attempting to love anyone else, we don't have to be completely healed and we don't have to perfect all these desired qualities within us. But don't expect some perfect person to come along and fulfill all your desires without you putting in work in on yourself first.

Dear Me, Dear You, Dear Us

Where are you

It seems as though I've been searching my entire life just to find you

There's been so many moments where I thought I did

Before even finding clarity of who you really are

Or who I wanted you to be

Who you were was far

Somewhere out in the distance

Maybe non existent

At least in my reality

Each time I experienced a moment that wasn't gifted with your arrival

I wanted to give up

Stop searching

Stop looking

And surrender.

Be

Lye Still

Eventually I did

Because the binoculars I carried with me this entire journey became all too heavy

Too pointless

Why drag along a device meant to show me the details in the external world

If I can't see

What can I see?

Is it me that I cannot see?

Or you?

Or us?

I see

it's me. .

It's me I see now

Seeing me helped me see

I never needed the binoculars

The search wasn't outside of me

But in me

In me I see

You

A reflection of my essence

My presence

In another form

Outside of me

You're out of me

But in me

Only appearing

Through my inner deep

Dive

Our energy

It's like synergy

No wonder those binoculars couldn't see these green eyes

It's not this physical illusion where the treasure lies

It's in the magic

I found in me

To see you

To see us

we

Are free

Dear Me, Dear You, Dear Us | Tyler A. Norman

Family

Energy repeats itself infinitely; high and even low vibrations go on (until they are alchemized). Our DNA is created by the DNA passed down from our mother and our father; DNA being made of energy. When a life forms, a singular cell combines with another until a human is created from trillions of combines cells. Essentially we are our parents, our grandparents, our kids, and everyone with which we share blood, we share similar energy. Think of it like this; when a male and female join to create a child, that child is a clone made from the same energies of the parents.

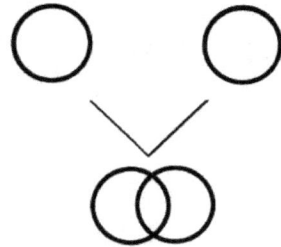

This happens continuously; parents have kids, the kids have kids, and so on. Everything having happened to our bloodline, if not healed, turned to high vibration, and released, those vibrations pass to us and as an energy within us; then that energy attracts similar events into our lives. Genetics even suggest we make the same decisions our parents would in the same situation. For example, if a parent was molested as a child yet kept it hidden, suppressed the emotions behind it, and never healed or released the event, that same energy which has been suppressed but still present is now in the DNA of the child. The child now carries such vibration, attracting a similar event into its life. The child may respond in the same way, out of fear, and suppress the event. Then the cycle repeats itself infinitely until someone heals and releases that energy from the bloodline.

This goes the same for drug use, depression, physical and verbal abuse, doing time, illnesses, and any form of low vibrations. We are our parents; our parents are us. We should also highlight the high vibration which pass down to us from our parents such as our humor, gifts, talents, and good looks.

Our families are gifted mirrors to us; open the gifts and start seeing the reflection of what needs healing. Any behavior we find bothersome from our family are only triggers to the wounds we need to heal inside of us as well. If your one who argues with your mom or dad constantly, consider the fact that your mirroring each other; triggering wounds present in both of you. Heal together. We are all mirrors continuously breeding new reflections. If you want your future kids to be love, create love within yourself first.

Our Mirrors are the Teachers

Life is a school, we are the student, and everything around us is our teacher. We are always learning lessons from the teachers around us. Just like in an actual school, if we don't learn the lessons our teachers try to show us, we have to repeat them. It's the same in real life; lessons we are meant to face will be repeated until they are learned. We must learn the entirety of it and not attempt to escape or it will simply reappear in a different form often harder and stronger. Different person; same lesson. When we try to ignore what the universe is telling us, universe sorta says "okay lil bitch.. you gone learn today, I'm gonna deliver you an even shittier situation or person till you fall flat on your face and learn your worth." Not in those words but in that energy.

"The people you meet are either reflections of a repeated cycle or guides toward a new start. Notice the difference."

-Unknown

When we do apply those lessons our mirrors have taught us, just like in education, those teachers will test us. Those teachers who relayed the lesson will present us with a test; depending on if we pass tells us if we have truly learned and applied the lesson to our daily life. If we do pass, then we know we are ready for the next grade level. I've had some mirrors I've learned my lessons and parted ways with make a reappearance in my life. Just when I thought everything had been learned, a mirror comes back to try me. In some situations, I've realized the test in front of me, held my composure, and responded with growth. Others, I've forgotten what I learned and went awf; a couple failed test have gotten me held back. But, that's okay, I just didn't learn the lesson fully yet, there's no timeline to growth. As long as we are growing we can move at whatever pace we need to.

When we really begin to look at life as a school, situations as lessons, and people as our teachers we can be more mindful of our present moment. Instead of reacting toward something, we can begin to see everything for what it is; a lesson to prepare us for the next level or a test. We have to be present so we can observe the mirrors around us. Then, we can use them to teach us things we need to work on or things we are really doing great at. It's all about perspective.

When we experience discomfort, it gives opportunity to learn growth. Pain gives opportunity to learn purpose. Anger allows us to learn compassion and forgiveness. Abandonment allows us how learn self-fulfillment and wholeness. Things we have no control over teaches us how to surrender. Certain addictions show us how to regain our power. Our triggers show us our wounds. Rejection teaches us faith and redirection. Fear teaches us to be courageous. Everything in life teaches us unconditional love.

Love your own reflection; use your mirrors as an opportunity to see a wound within yourself. See the triggers as a mirror for an internal wound; then love it and nourish it. Make it an opportunity to shower yourself in love. Others are here for us to understand and love ourselves right there in the reflection. We are all souls on a learning journey. We can help others on their journey while simultaneously furthering our own. Then, we can thank them for the lesson and at the same time thank ourselves for growing. See it this way and your unconditional love for yourself and others will reach a whole new depth. Heart chakra litty.

Nature

The universe is full of reflections; a bunch of mirrors all the same but different. Everything we see is a reflection of us at the core. One fractal mirrored itself time and time again creating infinite fractals which reflect back the one is what we call the universe. Just like our bloodline is a continuous breeding of new reflections; the universe is the same. We come from the ultimate source and higher power which is the universe; we are made of it. We all are a manifestation of earth, fire, water, and air continuously replicating. We are trillions of cells within the body of the earth; all mirrors, all connected, all one from the same source.

To remind us of the fact everything in the universe is a mirror to us sometimes nature shows us literal mirrors; when you look into a body of water, often delicately floating on the surface is a reflection. Sometimes we have to look deeper at Nature as a mirror. When we sink into the details we'll see we match natures patterns. Like lightning strikes and our nervous systems, tree trunk rings and our finger prints, tree branches and blood vessels. We have trillions of cells within us just like there are trillions of stars above us. We match the birth cycle of nature, we connect with the moons cycles, as well as yearly cycles as a planet. Everything is a pattern and everything is connected. We are a reflection of the universe. We are made in God's image.

"As above so below."
-Thoth

Nature is also mirror to show us traits in ourselves and help us learn lessons. Each plant, insect, animal, or any element in nature vibrates a certain frequency like all things in the universe. Those energies translate to different qualities to mirror a reflection of us. Nature is a mirror to us and our reaction to it is an awareness of us. Things we are afraid of in nature are a mirror to show us qualities of ourselves we are afraid to embrace. I used to have this deep disliking for rain; rain is water mirroring our emotional body. My past disliking of rain was a mirror to me being fearful of feeling my emotions flowing. Now that I embrace my emotions flowing, I embrace rain. I also was disgusted by ponds and lakes because I thought the water was dirty and nasty so I avoided it; ultimately out of fear. This reflects a mirror to me because I use to avoid and be disgusted by the murkiness in my emotional body, aka the low vibrating emotions that came through. Not realizing everything in life is equally beautiful. Another example; there's this spot in my backyard I always go to, for photos and other things. I feel comfortable there, one day while in this same spot I noticed the ground was sunk in a tad; but, I ignored it for quite some time. Then, finally after it rained I went to that same spot and stood in the sun. Suddenly the heel of my foot dug in revealing hollow ground underneath the surface. I felt a strong urge to dig into the ground to find out why it was hollow underneath; but a surge of fear overcame me. I feared if I would dig up a dead body, hit a wire, or get bit by a snake. I then realized my ignoring the sunken ground for so long and fear of digging to uncover the reason for the hollow ground was a mirror to me. I was unconsciously fearing grounding myself and digging deep within my roots to uncover the source of my internal holes; aka my childhood wounds. See how this works?

The things we love in nature are qualities we love in ourselves. I love a sunny day like no other; I also love my fiery energy. Remember this goes for plants, animals, insects, and all things in nature. People have spirit animals because those animals are ones they love and relate to; why? Because that animal has qualities similar to the person. See how everything is a mirror?

It's so important to spend time in nature to check up on your own energy. Go out and be present with the obliging vibrations of the universe; let them show you your energy. If you feel tense, fearful, or resistant toward nature it's a reflection of the energy you are currently carrying. Pay attention to how you react to certain things and study the qualities of those things which you reacted to. However you react to a certain vibration is a reflection of your inner world which aligns with it.

Inner Outer, Outer Inner

Look at the earth as a mirror to humanity. If we look at mother nature, we'll see she isn't thriving as she should; she's full of toxic chemicals and manmade materials. When we look at the reflection we'll see us in the same predicament; inner becomes outer. If the earth isn't healthy neither are we; outer effects inner.

We are one collective consciousness; we are life force god creations projecting illusions of similar realities. The differences in our reality depend on our own inner world; our own thoughts and emotions create our vibration. Those who vibrate the same stick together and experience almost identical realities; mirrors. Before we experience anything on the outside the inside must align. Our inner world is our outer world; they are mirrors. If we want true friends we must build a true friendship with our self. If we want real love, we must first fall in love with our self. If we want abundance, we must first feel abundant within. We must fill our minds with plentiful thoughts and fill our bodies with copious energies; foods which grow in abundance, like fruits and vegetables. I never really understood the whole health being wealth idea until recently when I studied the mirror concept. EVERYTHING is energy; to be wealthy is to have an abundance of different energies whether that be good food, money, possessions, or people. So, when we fill our body with high vibrational energy and plants that grow in abundance, we carry that energy in us. We become one with it and like a mirror it reflects all around us.

Pay attention to what you are reflecting. If we want a life full of happiness on the outside, we must first be truly happy inside without anything to do with the outside world. Don't continuously search for external remedies for an internal issue. We must constantly create love within for live a life never without. Just like we breathe in and out in a flowing motion, our energy flows in and out in the same motion.

We create a torus which is an infinite revolving energy. We are a spirit inside of a physical body, meaning our invisible inner world literally creates our physical world. Notice we breathe in first, then out; which suggest anything occurring outside started inside. When you face issues in the physical plane, always check in on the spiritual plane for the real root of the issue.

Imagine a T.V. projector; that little box is fully of things like beliefs, thoughts, and emotions. What it projects on the white wall is an illusion made up from all that's inside of it. If the things inside the box are based on fear; it will project a scary movie. If they are based on love it will project a fairy tale. We are the T.V. projectors and the white wall is our reality. Be love; live love.

Dreams

"Everyone in your dreams is you."
-Sigmund Freud | Neurologist, Psychoanalyst

Dream interpretation becomes a lot easier when you see others as a mirror to yourself. When we have dreams of people we just have to look at the person and figure out what part of us do they represent. For Example, if our ex-best friend pops up in our dream, this could be a signal we have not learned the lesson we needed to from that friendship. Or, we need to apply the lesson we did learn to a current waking life situation. Many times we'll even have dreams of animals, or natures elements as well. When we figure out what they mirrored to us, we can easier interpret what our dream is trying to tell us. Next time you have a dream with others you recognize, ask yourself, "what am I trying to show myself by creating this in my dream? What aspect of myself does this represent?". Write down your dreams, there are so many messages in them. The dreamland is the open canvas of the universe. Pay attention to the pictures being painted for you and be grateful

Losing Mirrors

There was a long period during my transformation I began losing a lot. My mirrors were all vibrating out. I felt so incredibly alone I wanted to cry all the time; I let myself cry because I knew there was a lesson in it all.

There were so many times I reminisced on my old relationships and how at the moment I wish I still had them and really missed them. A couple times I even hit them back up with FaceTime or a text and poured out all of my loving energy into them. Only to get a dry ass response back; still leaving me feeling alone. Losing mirrors was hard to swallow because there were some people I wanted so badly to grow with me. There were relationships I tried to hang onto that didn't clique the same. I even tried to share everything I learned with some, so they could be in my same head space. Hoping this would somehow make them stay; But they couldn't understand it because this was my own growth I had to experience.

A couple nights before a Libra full moon (Libra rules all relationships and full moons bring up emotions) I had this dream I was at a party hanging out. I saw a dog that belonged to this stranger and I went to go hug it; in my dream my intention was to use my touch to emit high vibrating love energy. But, to my surprise the dog turned rabid and tried to bite my hand off. In the dream I was so hurt and confused as to why the dog wanted to bite me when I was trying to love it. In waking life, the party represents the social scene and the dog represents loyalty and relationships. The dream was showing me how I keep trying to nourish the relationships with people who no longer belong in my life; if I keep trying to vibrate with old mirrors I'll keep feeling like I'm getting bit. Dreams are mirrors to us; so, really the dog biting me was me biting my own self in the ass by not letting go.

The thing about life is, everything is temporary; seasons, jobs, living situations, and even people in our lives. We find it so hard to let go of things because we think they are for us. When in reality we don't own anyone or anything, we just get to experience them for whatever amount of time the universe has planned out. Whether it's a conversation, an hour, a day, a few months, a decade, or the rest of this life.

I had to realize some relationships are only meant to last for a season and when that season is over I must focus on being grateful for experiencing their presence and not wallow in their absence. We have to focus on what is; when we continue crawling back to past situations like exes, old schools, old jobs, and toxic friendships, we block new energy from entering. At the same time, I had to learn that letting go of mirrors no longer meant to be in our lives doesn't mean blocking them, never speaking to them again, or holding grudges. Its surrendering, its loving people and places from a distance; wishing them growth and happiness throughout the rest of their journey. Its understanding our journeys no longer align but having an appreciation for them and all they have brought to our lives (lessons and blessings).

Losing mirrors also becomes difficult if we use them to fill a void. We tend to need people because we use them to fill something in us. But we forget that we already have the ability to tap into every energy we need in life within our own selves. Everything outside is just a reflection of what's already there. Remember the things we love about someone are already within us, they just remind us and help us see those things. But when we associate them with something outside of ourselves or as something we need to fill up an empty space. We will continuously feel like we're losing ourselves when our mirrors move on. It's okay to mourn the loss of who we were when we once vibrated in tune with a mirror. But know we can't lose something if we are already everything. We are the universe expressing itself; unlimited. When we recognize we're whole, we can peacefully surrender to people coming and going in and out our lives. Because it's not a loss it's just a change of season.

Losing mirrors only means gaining new ones; but, we must let go, be open, and receiving. As long as we are growing and aligning with our authentic self, no matter how many mirrors we lose we must remember those old mirrors were never meant to grow with us on this new level; they were a teaching lesson to help get us here. Because I began learning the lessons my mirrors showed me, there were people who I simply just didn't vibe with anymore and places I had to leave. Which means I have vibrated out of that energy I was once in. That mirror has shown me my reflection and I have learned the lesson; time to move on to the next grade level. We can't be afraid or feel guilty about outgrowing some of the people and environments around us, we won't outgrow whatever is meant to be in our life; it will grow with us. When we change our energy, our mirrors will meet us at a new level or they will vibrate out. It's not easy to leave someone or be left, but know we are not bound to people forever.

The reality is, not everyone is meant to come with us to new levels in our journey. Those mirrors that grow with us in vibration; those are our tribe. Our people; the ones who are meant to rock with us through this learning journey for now. And often, old mirrors come back around after divinely guided separation has allowed each individual to heal on their own path. However, we must understand the meaning of truly appreciating the mirrors in our lives. Many of us experience ownership and expectation from our mirrors instead of appreciation. Ownership is picking the flower from its roots, holding it, and keeping it for self-satisfaction. Appreciation is leaving the flower where it should be, where it will continue to grow with nature. Yet, appreciating the fact we get to experience its presence in this season, even if it's temporary. We have to embrace the fact that people in our lives are only temporary, we don't own them. People come and go; after all, life does go in cycles. We must get used to the flow.

This lesson was hard for me to learn, so it repeatedly itself many times. After several of these universal lectures, I decided instead of drowning in the idea of being lonely I had to embrace the solitude and try to understand what it was teaching me. I knew solitude was not permanent; it was divine timing between losing mirrors and gaining new ones. There was something I was supposed to be doing during this time of isolation...

Activity 1

Mirror Check

- Make a chart for as many people in your life as you desire. Ask yourself the following.

What do I love about this person?	What bothers me about this person?

Activity 2

Parental Control

- Make another chart for your parent(s).
- List ways you mirror your mother/father and ways your mother/father mirrors you.
- Dig deep, list the dark and light you reflect in each other.
- Physically (traits, health), mentally (habits, conditions, beliefs, fears, love), emotionally (suppressed emotions, relationship with emotions), and Spiritually (passion, gifts).

I my mother	My mother is me

I am my father	My father is me

Activity 3

Reflections

Try a unique exercise used all over for deepening relationships.

1. Stare into another person eyes for 4 minutes straight. (One with some sort of relation to you, or a stranger if you prefer).

2. If you look into the glare of another person's eyes you will see a reflection of yourself, you'll see what they see.

3. Reflect on what that means to you.

Chapter 9
Solitude

The Road to Solitude

Sounds scary right? I'm not even going to fake it; it is. The reason we fear this state is because we know the truth will be revealed and we will have a choice to take action on the answers we get or we will stay the same. Though scary, it is the most beautiful, addicting, and enlightening state of all time.

Solitude is a place where we are stripped away from all things around us, this way we can go within to uncover what it is we need to heal. In solitude, our wounds and shadows can rise to the surface where they can be felt, healed, and released. Solitude is not loneliness, it is a space for deep healing and connection with self. I've faced several periods of isolation in the past few years of my life. I'll start from the beginning when I finally opened myself up to what solitude had to show me.

I had about a month of gap time between the end of my summer internship and the fall semester of my junior year in college. All year I had been working to boss up my business and grow as a person. I figured, since I had extra time, I'd pick up a few habits to further my personal growth. I detoxed some of my social media, cut back on watching Tell-a-Vision, skipped on going out, and started meditating.

Meditation

I committed to mediating morning and night. At first, I sat in silence and repeated affirmations in my head until ten minutes was up. As time went on, I started to further explore the aspects of meditation. I focused on just being; practicing becoming aware of each energy body. Bringing my awareness to my breath, letting it go deep, and flow in and out. Checking in on the physical sensations of my body; at times I focused on the energy of crystals in my hands or if I felt any aches or pains, I assessed them. I let my thoughts flow to see where my mental energy was at; catching negative ones that popped up and practiced transmuting them to positive. I allowed myself to feel what emotions were present. The more I practiced meditation the more I was able to move through each energy body; cleansing them. The deeper I went, I entered a trance like state where I was floating in nothingness. Similar to floating out in the cosmos, in total darkness yet consumed with peace. Always coming back with a piece to the puzzle.

Sometimes, I practiced just being open to receiving a message through thoughts, imagines, symbols, emotions, or colors etc. Meditation was spending time with my true self. I could no longer run away from the thoughts I distracted myself from; it was me and my rawness. Without distractions, opinions, influences, or comparisons from the outside world; I started hearing my inner voice. The solitude and stillness of meditation allowed me to spend time with my spirit. The saying "know thyself" became real. I was able to put so many pieces of the puzzle together from my past to present. This became a drug; addicting. I had a desire to understand more with little interest in what was going on in the outside world. I was learning so much within myself.

"When you pray, you speak to god; when you meditate, you listen."

-Unknown

God communicates to us through energies like signs, colors, emotions, and thoughts; not human language. When meditating, we can better understand whatever the universe is trying to tell us. It is a place where we dive deep within ourselves and find the many answers we long for. Not to mention, our frequency instantly rises when we meditate. Tap in.

There were many times I was reluctant to mediate because my ego didn't want to face the lesson being communicated to me; our ego lives in our comfort zone. However, our spirit loves meditation; it loves when we let it guide us. When you experience a resistance, like your body saying, "bih, I'm hungry let's get up", it's your ego. Reluctance to meditate is fear of the ego and not our spirit. Which means, dig a little deeper because there's something to uncover.

Intuition

That little voice in the back of my head started getting louder and louder; I was listening closely. That gut feeling became more prevalent. I realized my intuition was God, my own inner goddess, my angels, and ancestors speaking to me; helping me make my next move. Like an inner GPS guiding me toward the right direction and the right answers on my path. These spirits whispered; but with the practice of stillness, observation, and meditation, my mind was quiet enough to hear. Listening to my intuition pushed me to make the single greatest and scariest decision in my existence. I dropped out of college and changed the direction of my life. The way I was living was not in alignment with my true self anymore. It was time for me to begin creating a new reality in line with my desires. I couldn't explain it to anyone, all I knew was that my inner voice told me to start creating my new life. My spiritual energy craved authenticity.

Meeting True Solitude

After I made this huge decision, it felt as if my life was in shambles. I lost so much; friends, opportunities, and comfort. I let go of the most familiar part of my everyday life; school. I moved back home and a huge shift took place. I had no routine, no schedule, no meetings, no job, and no idea what I was doing. With no one to talk to about the inner turmoil going on inside my head and nothing to keep me busy; I met true solitude. This gave me no choice but to dive deeper into my spirit and let it lead the way.

My spirit led me to total isolation. In order to grow I had to stripped down to the very core of my essence. I had to be left with nothing to realize

I'm something without anything. I had to learn to love myself as just Tyler in my imperfect rawness. Not loving me because of my friends, my accomplishments, my titles, my clothes, or anything outside of me; but, to love me for who I was on the inside. I'm so grateful God took away all those things from me so I could realize who I was deep down and begin building a solid foundation of love from the root up.

In order to truly heal and face our inner demons, solitude is absolutely necessary. We need time to hear our own spirit inside; without outside voices talking over us, so we can continue to walk in our destined path. Solitude is where we begin to truly love ourselves for everything we are, not everything we have. It is the hidden place of greatness.

Alignment

Although I was losing everything, it somehow felt as though it would all be worth it. Everything was so tragic but peaceful at the same time. I felt more of myself than ever, more connected to my authentic self and my divine path. Cutting out outside negative energy, spending time with myself in meditation, getting to knowing myself, and listening to my intuition caused a shift in my vibration. The universe was taking away things, people, and situations that weren't meant to be in this new cycle of my life. Solitude lead to my rebirth, **spiritual awakening**, and new life. This was only the beginning.

Activity

Face Yourself

1. Put away your phone.
2. Put down all outside world distractions.
3. Sit in silence. You can choose to close your eyes or keep them open.
4. Get comfortable being in solitude, take time to be with yourself.
5. Let your thoughts flow.
6. Try not avoid emotions; cry if you need to.
7. Ask your body what it needs.
8. Ask your spirit to come out and guide you.
9. Repeat everyday

Chapter 10 Spiritual Awakening

What is a Spiritual Awakening?

The term spiritual awakening sounds like a burst of magic in one's life, that transforms them into a beautiful butterfly! I'll agree that's the after math; but, no butterfly is released without being stuck in a dark and lonely cocoon for a while. A cocoon where we can't see much light; only a space for growth and transformation. It's all a process and a cycle.

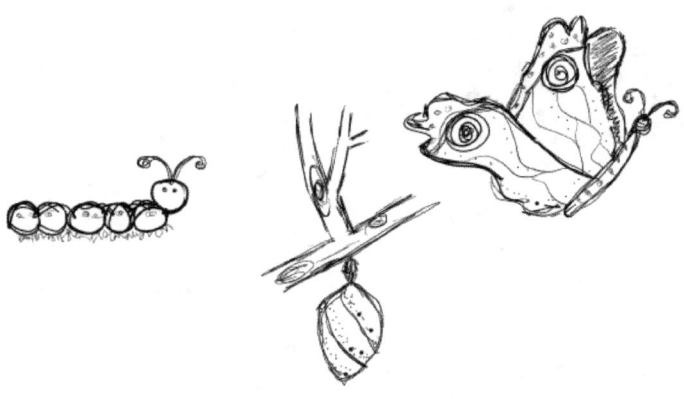

Sometimes I think of it as a rebirth, a glow up, or an awakening. Regardless, true spiritual growth is a process of destruction. Each person's spiritual awakening is unique; the depth of it is directly connected to the degree of pain and amount of trauma that person has faced in life. From my experience and intuition, I believe a spiritual awakening includes the resurfacing of wounds, traumas, and pains. All those that have been suppressed, still cause emotional distress, and continue creating blockages within the heart. The pain we've learned from and accepted is not the issue, it is all the things we learned to cover up and ignore. This requires deep soul work, along with digging up and breaking down darkness in one's life. Then, using that darkness to learn our lessons, learn unconditional love, and become a light within ourselves.

A spiritual awakening is alchemy; dissolve and coagulate. In order to solve we must break down each of our traumas. *Solve et coagula*; meaning breakdown and separate in order to combine all elements back into a new higher form.

Open The Heart

You may be thinking, why it gotta be all that? Which is exactly what I was thinking at the time of mine. But, after my own awakening and gaining a whole new perspective. I believe in the chakra system; different points of energy within us. The chakras are associated with certain frequencies. We danced around this a little earlier; let's go deeper. If you were to take a prism and hold it up to the sun light, RA which is the source of energy on earth, it would reflect seven colors. The seven colors in the rainbow which vibrate at certain frequencies of light. These are the colors we can see with the human eye and also the seven energy points within the human body. If you were to take that prism with sunlight and angle it toward a human body; there we have the chakras. The lower chakras including; the root, sacral, and solar plexus are associated with the physical world. These are the first few chakras to be developed for any life form. We grow from the root and up; making the root chakra the first one. For plants, the root begins in mother earth, which is a representation of the physical (remember earth = physical energy). For humans, the root starts to grow in the mother's physical body. Once a plant begins to grow it can then move from the roots toward the sun; we know the element of fire equals spiritual energy. For humans, once we develop an opening and balance of these physical chakras we can then move on to the higher chakras, the spiritual world. Aka, a spiritual awakening, glow up, and meeting of higher chakras. **#Naturalisthewaytoglow**

Chakras	
Crown (Purple) –Knowing Third Eye (Indigo)– Seeing Throat (Blue)– Expressing **Heart (Green) – Loving** Solar Plexus (Yellow) –Doing Sacral (Orange) –Feeling Root (Red) – Grounding	CROWN THIRD EYE } SPIRITUAL THROAT HEART BALANCE SOLAR PLEXUS SACRAL } PHYSICAL ROOT

This is why I call it a glow up. I see it as a literal rise in high frequency glowing energy moving up our energy points; from root to crown. But, before we can move from the lower to higher chakras we must get through the heart chakra. The middle and balance between the two worlds. We are a spirit having a physical experience on earth; our heart is the center point. It is what's keeping our spirit alive in human form. It is the organ and the energy point which pumps life force energy throughout our entire body. Our heart is also what creates the electromagnetic field around us; aka our aura. The energy others can pick up on just by being in range. We can feel a heavy heart in the aura of those round us; at least that's how it is for me. The heart chakra holds energy of unconditional love, balance, and harmony when it's open. Then, feelings of resentment, trauma, and pain when not. Keeping our aura and our entire reality lit requires getting through the heart chakra, opening it, and filling it with unconditional love for self and others. An open and clutter free heart chakra allows us to give and receive unconditional love in an infinite motion of energy. We often wonder why we can't attract and experience forms of love, it's because it's not able to flow through us, we can't give it or receive it with a close off heart. So, if we have some shit heavy on our heart we haven't come to terms with, we have to face it before we can truly grow. The condition of the heart effects the condition of our reality. If we don't face these painful experiences and traumas and we hold them all inside they will manifest into our reality and in our body as physical pain. Everything physical starts as a spiritual, emotional, and mental energy first then turns physical. Just like any creation; everything is invisible before it ever becomes physical. Same with trauma and pain. Hopefully this is all coming together for you.

Release the Pain

The parts of our body we experience these energetic pains turned to physical are linked to the seven energy points in our body; the chakras. Each is located at a specific point in the body and connects with all organs in those areas. The pains we feel in those areas are often low vibrating energy left there. We can learn what type of energy it is by looking at the chakras. For instance, one who has heart issues holds low vibrating energy in their heart; from the things they eat that disrupts the heart function and also pains they haven't let go in the heart. The actual heart as an organ connects with the heart chakra, which deals with unconditional love for self and others. Some of the low vibrating energy there could be a resentment or hate toward someone else or ourselves. When we keep low vibrations here, we can experience chest pains, breast cancer, problems breast feeding our children, or literally die from a broken heart. No wonder heart disease is the leading cause of death; we live in a society that carries low vibrations in the heart.

"Our bodies tell trauma stories using the language of symptoms"
- **Unknown**

Another example; painful periods stem from the uterus. The uterus is associated with the sacral chakra which is associated with emotional flow, intimacy, closeness, and creativity. I know this because I've had personal experience; those extremely painful period cramps are low vibrations and blockages in the sacral chakra. As women we experience more emotion than men, it is in our nature. Because of this extra emotional energy, mother nature gifted us with a way of release. A way of naturally releasing emotions through our sacral chakra; many times in synch with the feminine energy of the moon. We call it a period; just like water and emotional energy we have a flow. Like myself, many women experience heavy flow and painful cramping during our emotional release. This points to low vibrational energy flowing through the sacral. Statistically speaking many women of color are marketed to and advised to be placed on birth control to deal with these issues. Birth control creates mucus in the cervix, often disrupts, and in my case stops the flow of blood and emotions; further suppressing energy which needs to be released. Any suppressing of all those low vibrations in the sacral can cause endometriosis, infertility, or more painful periods.

Next, headaches and migraines have to do with our crown chakra.

There are many different symptoms and attributes as to why we can experience a blocked crown chakra; but, I'm certain all the toxic hair products and relaxers being placed on our crown don't help. I notice a huge difference in my connection with spirit when my hair is not nourished. Especially when I put on some bullshit product; I feel disconnected and heavy. Then there's thyroid issues which are pains derived from a blocked throat chakra; an inability to express one's truth. Us women are often silenced. But, I'll stop there I'm sure you get the point. Holding onto low vibrations rooted in fear will cause us to rot from the inside out. Then, create the vibration and DNA of our children.

"Every woman who heals herself helps heal all the women that came before her and all those who come after."
- Unknown

Live with Heart

I've mentioned repeatedly, every person in our lives is a teacher. Every situation we face, minor or extreme, is a teaching moment. These people and situations were purposely placed in our lives at that exact moment for us to grow, find our purpose, and find light. Unfortunately, we haven't been taught to deal with our traumas as they are right in front of us. So, we must dig up everything we ve buried in order to be in alignment with our path. First, we dig up these low vibrations; then, learn our soul lessons from them. Finally, we can turn that low energy into something positive. Increasing our own well-being and high vibrations. That's how you grow, evolve, and live a purposeful life. You have to get to know the darkness and pain before you can appreciate the light.

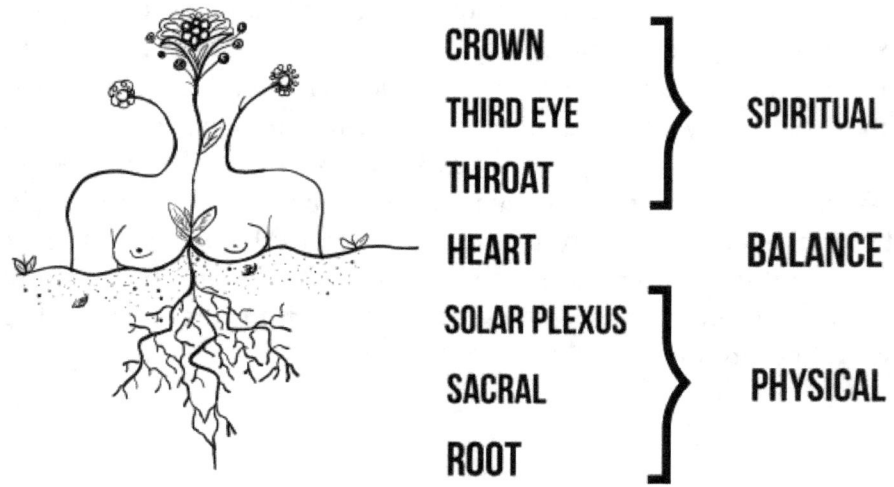

CROWN
THIRD EYE   } SPIRITUAL
THROAT

HEART   BALANCE

SOLAR PLEXUS
SACRAL   } PHYSICAL
ROOT

Ya'll know I like metaphors and believe everything around us is a mirror. So let's compare this to a flower. We are all flower seeds; destined for a life full scenery and beauty in the future. The flowers don't just appear; they are planted as seeds. Planted in dirt and darkness. This little seed with so much potential, must gain its nutrients from the womb of mother earth; the physical world. Then, it must burst through the seed and push past the darkness until it sees light. Only then, can the flower grow to its full potential and serve its purpose. The same is with us when we are literally born for the first time. Then, again when we experience a rebirth, glow up, or spiritual awakening. You can pick your own name for it at this point.

Bursting open the heart chakra can be extremely painful exactly how child birth is painful and the seedling bursting through the soil is painful. But, what comes out on the other side is breathtaking and every bit worth it. The heart chakra is how we learn to love unconditionally; when we learn to love can we truly learn to live.

Disclaimer

With all of this being said, everything is from my perspective. The best thing is all of our perspectives are allowed to be different and change as we wish. All of our spiritual experiences are different. That doesn't make any of them weird, over the top, or any less than our own. Enjoy your own connection to God and the spiritual world; what's important is you connect with it in the best way **you** can. For me that was exploring my curios ty and finding out what I believed in my own spirit. Fear is a low vibraticn; so I didn't let it confine me and get in the way. Then, I found even more love within myself as I learn to balance unconditional love in my physical, mental, emotional, and spiritual energies. In no way am I telling anyone what they should or shouldn't believe in. The purpose of me sharing this next chapter is to encourage everyone to explore every aspect of themselves. There, we can understand who we are in every form and begin to love ourselves fully. We know what happens when we love ourselves fully.

Activity

The first step to healing is accepting.

- Go back to your puzzle pieces; examine the painful experiences you wrote down (add more if you'd like).
- Reflect on childhood traumas, wounds, and resentment you have toward others; accept them as low vibrating energies needing to be released.

Chapter 11
My Awakening

My Spiritual Awakening

After giving my perspective of what an awaking is; hopefully this will help others connect to or understand my own spiritual awakening. I mentioned in my other chapter, Solitude, prior to my awakening I made the decision to begin meditating. In meditation I was able to get in touch with my raw and truest self. I was able to quite my mind to hear the spirits in and around me. This way I could experience my own spiritual awakening. I didn't plan on awakening or choose to experience it; it's not a part of everyone's purpose on earth. But, little did I know it was always in my path; my ancestors chose me. I was always meant to awaken because it was a piece to my puzzle.

At the time of my spiritual glow up, I didn't really understand what was happening to me. All I wanted to do was better myself and grow as a person; which is why I tried out mediation. I wasn't planning on being in total isolation or even becoming spiritual. Quite frankly, I didn't even know what being spiritual meant. I had a close relationship with God, but in a different way. Due to my ignorance in the process I felt as if my life was falling to crumbs; completely dissolving to pieces.

"No tree it is said, can grow to heaven unless its roots reach down to hell."
- Carl Jung | Psychiatrist

In order to go through this glow up we must dig deep down and start at the roots of everything. Starting at our root chakra then rising up like a Phoenix to our crown. Like a flower, in order to grow, we must bloom where we are planted. All circumstances leading to my awakening landed me right back in my soil. After being away for two years seeing my outer reflections, I was divinely placed back into my childhood home along with my family right where everything began; at the roots. This way I could be expose to the energy all childhood trauma, coping mechanisms, and conditioned beliefs developed from the beginning. In order to heal myself on a deeper level I needed to return home to see my mirrors which reflect the deepest parts of me. Many people try to run away from their roots; there home town, where life began, because it's a trigger. There, it is a reminder of the childhood trauma they experienced and continue running away from. But, we can't keep running.

Dissolving Conditioned Belief Systems

As I said previously, I had a close relationship with God. I knew there was a spirit within me; whatever it was. I classified myself under one religion because it was my only perspective from where I was at in life. Since childhood, my healthily curious mind questioned everything for more understanding. I felt a spirit but, I always carried an urge to go further than the particular box of understanding I had. However, my religion had a level of fear over me. I refused to listen to any person of a different opinion because I didn't want to hear anything that made me question my way of life; deep down I was afraid.

On a serious note we all know how the game telephone goes. There's a real story at the beginning but each ear it enters hears and understands it differently; everyone's perception of the story changes. I think most religions are an extension of universal truth; spirituality and energy being the center of it all. All having a higher power/ God, a way of connecting with it, a figure which has resurrected or is a savior, an interpretation of creation, and/or a way of living life. Using similar symbols of the snake, bird, spiral, the eye, feminine and masculine energy etc. Due to various reasons, I believe most religions are attempting to understand and teach the same thing; enlightenment, love, morality, spirituality, and living a meaningful life; whatever that may be. It's as if someone asked what is the meaning of life in a game of telephone and each religion is each person's explanation. All sounding different but ultimately rooting from the same thing.

There's an art museum where I live which presents various exhibits of artwork separated by culture, location in the world, and time period. It ranges from "Egyptian" to Greek, Roman, African, Chinese etc. Through being present and immersing myself into the stories of the art, I've noticed everything is an expression. All the artwork, the sculptures, hieroglyphics, paintings, pottery, and symbols express their perspective of creation, life, and the universe itself. Each borrowing symbols and attributes of the story before them.

"Don't be satisfied with stories, how things have gone with others. Unfold your own myth."
-*Rumi | Poet, Theologian, Jurist*

In religion, I see perspective. There's a reach for love, wisdom, and understanding of life. Yet, I think many have been clouded with human error. Religions are a man-made roadmap to a way of life; us humans tend to pollute things we create. A way of life that calls for separation, disapproval, in-acceptance, the death in afterlife, or death in waking life of all those outside of it is not a religion based on unconditional love. This is an attempt of love polluted with legalism, politics, separatism, fear, and idolization; human error derived from the ego.

That's not to say I despised religion or denied everything about it. There are beautiful practices, powerful teachings, and great wisdom in so many. With it, we learn to have faith in the unseen. My former religion led me here, it was a start to something infinitely deep. My spirit was just ready to carry me the rest of the way. As uncomfortable and gut wrenching as it was at first, overtime I let go of past beliefs. All along I was waiting on an external power to do magical work for me; when the true power had to be realized and activated within me. I became aware of the fact fear is a tactic to prevent spiritual exploration; it being the driver which prevents thinking outside of certain boxed ways of life. Fear being what holds us captive in our comfort zone, causes us to dehumanize other humans equal to us, and what brings up energy the opposite of love.

If everything is energy and energy is infinite did life really start or just evolve? Personally, with all the stories left behind by those before us, I think everything just gained inspiration from another and evolved. We evolved from the infinite energy of nature to different forms of life. Us still being made of the energy within nature. Let me go ahead and mention one more time, this is all my own perspective which may not be another person's truth. But, the way I see it is everything keeps coming back to energy; water, fire, earth, air, the sun, moon, and stars. From my own research I believe the first documented story was told by the first civilization manifested directly out of those energies; the ancient Khemitic energies. Everything after is a replication with replaced parts and personal perspectives added in.

The spirituality in our roots was not the religion forced upon our enslaved ancestors as a fear tactic. It was a realization of the kingdom of God within us, an interconnection with nature, the use of all natures elements for further elevation, a bond with our deceased ancestors, and other light spirits all around us. This type of connection to spirit is powerful; it will change the entire perspective and reality of its partaker. It's no wonder it was stripped away; spiritual enslavement.

After letting go of past limiting beliefs, I listened to my spirit instead of word of mouth. My soul is pure love and truth; it will never lead me astray. So, I followed what it whispered to my physical, mental, emotional, and spiritual energy and it led me to where I am today. When I listened to the whispers of my spirit I found God within myself. Not as a person, place, or thing; but, life, love, source, masculine and feminine, creation, and the entire universe.

"I looked in temples, churches, and mosque but I found the divine within my heart."

-Rumi | Poet

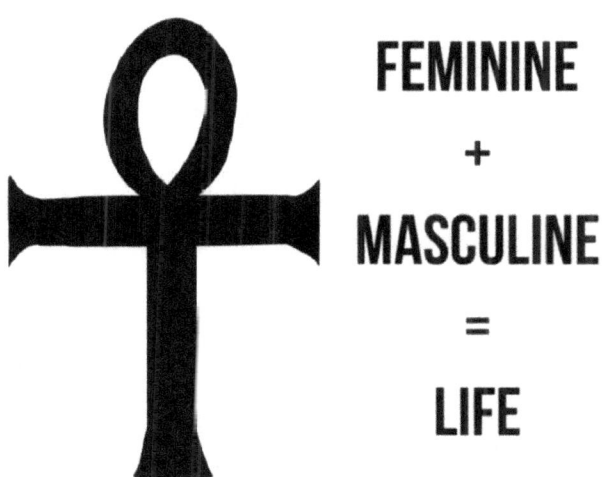

FEMININE

+

MASCULINE

=

LIFE

ANKH

Free spiritual beings are allowed to explore. I no longer let religion confine me because there's no limit; a wise man knows he will never know everything. Which means, knowledge is infinite and there are no definite answers. Though we may have great philosophies and spiritual practices to connect us in incredible ways, we will never know all the answers out there. Basing our entire life on one belief system, convinced it's absolute truth, and nothing else is a possibility is like a fish swimming in the broad ocean; yet confined to a fish tank. Yes, the fish is able to see the vast ocean; a ginormous world with millions of species and undiscovered territory. Yet, the with all of the beauty surrounding it, the fish is enclosed in a tank; unable to explore all that's out there. Stuck in the four walls it's limited to; four manmade walls. When we are free spiritual beings the glass walls of the tanks shatter. We are a fish free to uncover all the ocean has to offer; we have infinite discoveries to unlock. After all, 95% of the ocean is undiscovered.

I believe understanding creation is more than anything our human brains can even comprehend. Not everyone will agree with me here but that's okay. I choose to look at life with an open mind; willing the uncover as much about it as I can without limits. Everything I've been taught may not be the exact truth or maybe there's no absolute truth. Maybe everything is just prospective; I based my life off my own perspective. I learned to tap into my own perception of life, my own gut, and connection to spirit. The best thing about this type of freedom within self is I can fearless study all philosophies and spiritual practices to expand my mind on such a deeper level. This means I can travel the world, learn all the different perspectives of life, and engage in all cultures and practices; with no fear. This means adventure, knowledge, and freedom.

"A mind that is stretched by a new experience can never go back to its old dimensions."
-Oliver Wendell Holmes Sr. | Physician

I can take what symbols, practices, and understandings I resonate with to create my own way of life. There doesn't have to be a wrong or right way; I just take with me what feels like my truth. Also, I don't have to firmly believe in one thing; locking down my way of life doesn't feel like growth to me. Me keeping an open mind, knowing I'll never know everything, yet continuing to expose myself to knowledge and creating my own truths is growth. That's just a personal opinion. Whatever we believe is what we create in our reality. We literally create this illusion of reality within our own minds. Why place limits on the reality we can experience? I encourage everyone to gain inspiration from the religions, cultures, and civilization you most resonate with, then use your own understanding, intuition, and life experience to create your own story.

As long as we are living in unconditional love which is the highest frequency and essence of who we are, we can never be wrong.

This deeper connection with God, myself, and sudden acceptance of all types people in the world allowed me to push through the remainder of my awakening. I started to see the light in all the darkness. My seed was growing, my heart was beginning to open, but only scratching the surface.

Heal Thyself - Heart Chakra

There's this idea when you have money, a house, family, and food on your table you have nothing to ever be sad about. I think this idea is something I hid behind to resist my own trauma for a long time. I thought, I'm so fortunate in so many areas of my life, there really isn't anything I should feel hurt about. It was like, accepting the fact I had pain made me somewhat ungrateful for all I did have. Yes, these are blessing to have; but, no matter how much anyone has we all still face trauma. That's just a part of duality; with every blessing is a lesson.

For a long time, my heart chakra was closed. For various reasons, I had felt abandoned by multiple people, I witnessed emotionally toxic and abusive relationships, and I didn't want to experience any of this again. So, my protection mechanism was to close that part of myself off. I kept people at a distance; that way no one could leave a deep whole in me or try to get closer to me. I shut people out of my true inner world. There was no balance of feminine and Masculine energy within my heart. I wanted to give love but I blocked myself from receiving in fear of it being ripped away. As difficult as it was to let go of past belief systems. I had not yet felt the real depth of my awakening. This is when things became really unnerving. Here we were, finally bursting open the heart chakra; piece by piece.

The internal purging was the process of digging up traumas and suppressed wounds; those of which were still effecting my emotions and causing blockages in my heart. Here, I could reevaluate them within this new vibration in order to turn them to light. When I say shit hit the fan, shit smacked that fan. Childhood trauma and suppressed blockages I didn't even know were there came to make their presence known. There was a period of time when I cried every single day. I remember thinking to myself, "if I make it out of this, I'm going to be stronger than ever". I began the long healing process of deep internal wounds and I learned many hard lessons; lessons that changed me entirely. These lessons allowed me to let go of a lot of resentment in my heart. All the low vibrations I held in myself due to hurt from others had to be released. I had to forgive every person in my life I felt hurt by and see myself in the picture to understand what these lessons were trying to teach me.

Earlier I mentioned how we all have holes; these pains and trauma we experience are what causes the wholes inside of us. But, instead of healing from the inside, we try to look for filling from the outside. These outside fillers, aka band aids, will work at first but eventually the wound will keep bleeding through the band aid. The wound won't heal until we treat it properly.

One of many amazing lessons I learned about myself is I've been gifted with is abandonment; specifically, the feeling of being left for someone more important. Throughout my life I unconsciously tried to replace the person who caused this whole inside me. At first, it seemed like I was able to, the whole stopped bleeding for a bit. But eventually the exact same scenario repeated itself; someone more important came along, I felt abandoned, and there I was open and bleeding again. I kept replacing the band aid though. Throughout opening my heart chakra, I finalized saw this pattern of me continuing to try to fill this void within me through other people and being triggered when the same thing kept happening. The universe kept trying to show me my lesson but I wasn't paying attention. I realized I had to heal this wound with my own love and not the love from someone else.

By the way, abandonment or childhood trauma can be as simple as your best friend in kindergarten not talking to you anymore. It's still pain, even more as a kid. The experiences we have as kids cause us to develop self-protection mechanisms growing up; though we might not see them play out. For example, losing your best friend in kindergarten will have you holding onto a fear of abandonment; you might be jealous of a friend's friend thinking they might leave you for that other friend. Or, you might hold on to shitty friends because you don't want to feel that loss again. All things we do as adults are self-protection mechanism we've created from experiencing hurt and fear as children. We all have childhood trauma we dealt with as a kid; big or small these traumas repeat themselves in our adult life again and again until we heal the root of when the trauma first started.

Not only does our own trauma show up for healing, but the unhealed trauma passed down from our ancestors. We are made from invisible energy like thoughts, ideas, and beliefs mix with physical matter. All of these energies spiritual, mental, emotional, and physical come from our parents. Meaning, we are both our mothers and our fathers and they are their mothers and fathers; the cycle repeats infinitely. The black community comes from a history of slavery which has caused deeply rooted trauma in all of us; because of this historic and present day hatred toward our people, black family issues run deep.

Fear is the lowest vibration; it transforms into low vibrational behaviors such drug abuse, sexual abuse, verbally and physically abusive relationships, alcoholism, infidelity, abandonment, absent fathers, daddy issues, family secrets, feuds and drama at all the family functions. Then you have the members who are runners from family issues and live in a different city every year. All of this trauma causing us to separate from our own kin. We all have family and friends who seem like their lives are cursed; constantly facing trials and rough times. People getting killed, getting sick, having financial crisis, and getting locked up. All of these unfortunate events are not a curse; everything is a cycle of energy. Low vibrations from external forces, conditioning, and generational wounds repeating themselves and attracting more fear and death. We must break the cycle and truly live. Once we recognize the cycle and attempt to heal those wounds we are already changing the direction of the next generation. If you've already had children before beginning to heal your wounds. Don't worry, the change in behavior from your own healing will still have a positive effect on the child; as they watch how we move to develop human behaviors; DNA records behavior.

Sometimes we recognized the cycle and attempt to heal it through an outside outlet; giving the opposite treatment of what we experienced to a person in our lives. This is still healing and still a realization of trauma. But truly the most impactful healing starts within the self; releasing the pain, within the self. We must get to know ourselves, our true history, and heal our roots. It's our decision of whether or not we will choose to be victims of our circumstances and continue going down a path of destruction, or if we will keep pushing. Forgiveness and healing is done in layers; it takes time and patience to heal piece by piece. Once we think we've healed something we have just peeled back a layer and are getting to the deeper root of the issue. Have patience, it's important we know we aren't just healing our own wounds; but, our mothers, our mother's mothers, our father's, uncles, and aunts. We are healing all generational wounds passed down to us. As long as we keep going forward; we are still healing. Be the change in your family line. Be who you needed your parents to be. Be who your kids need you to be. Regardless, the energy you carry within will keep manifesting into not only your reality but will replicate into the reality of your offspring; it's our choice what energy we decide to pass on.

"When we heal ourselves, we heal our ancestors from wounds that run deep in our family. When we heal our ancestors we heal the world from wounds that run deep in humanity"

- **Miriam rose**

Fair warning this is the part you will want nothing more than to just crawl back to your space of comfort. You will feel extremely lost and uncomfortable; life is meant to be uncomfortable. You may feel out of touch, crazy, or like your falling apart. It's because you are; first dissolve then coagulate. To build your way back up you must first fall apart. No matter how scary, unfamiliar, and isolated this place might be, know on the other side is so much beauty and light. Be the flower. Push through darkness, light a fire underneath your ass, and fight; we are warriors in life's battle. At the same time, have patience and love for yourself as you have entered a tremendously brave journey.

Forgiveness – Heart Chakra

During this time, I gained a lot of love and forgiveness. I opened my eyes with a level of compassion for others. I thought how people have so much heavy shit on their hearts they are not releasing. Years of carrying around wounds and continuing to face new ones. Hurt people hurt people. I had to realize others weren't trying to hurt me, their pain was overflowing. I also had to cut out the idea of what I assumed people should have been for me. We as a society are conditioned to create these expectations of what people should act like. We have these ideas of what our fathers should do for us; bring us flowers and kiss our boo boos. What our friends should do for us; bring us soup when were sick and keep all our secrets. When everyone is who they are; not what we expect them or need them to be for us. A lot of my hurt rooted in my family and friends; I had this fairytale idea of what these figures should have been for me in my life. When they weren't that, I felt hurt and abandoned. My expectations only led to disappointment. First, I had to see I was depending on outside forces to make me feel loved and full inside. Then, I needed to understand the people who left my life or who didn't play the role I wanted them to, were not meant to; they were not a piece to my puzzle and it was time for me to stop crying about what was never meant to be. That was a tad harsh but sometime I had to be that way. I had this revelation of finally understanding all people have their own pain and their own journey in life; they can only be what they are and not everything others need or want them to be.

It's easier to forgive people for reflecting petty ass things to us. But, being in a position where a such tremendous amount of pain is inflicted that the idea of ending a life starts to fill the mind, is where the real test of the heart comes. Many of us colored folk experience so many moments based on survival. Moments where revenge and protective instincts come to high gear. Someone has harmed the people closest to us, blood or not. That anger, that resentment, that darkness that creeps in is heavy. It can completely cloud our mental and turn the heart cold.

I've been through a traumatic experience which caused me to enter straight savage mode. I had nightmares every night and my thoughts were dark. For a minute, I wasn't fucking with no love and light shit. But I'm here to say, that anger can turn to love and compassion that flows through our entire being and opens back up the heart. Allowing life force and warmth to fill our bodies again. Believe me when I say, what goes around comes the fuck right back around. Let's spirit handle the revenge and keep your energy within free from the bullshit.

"How others treat us is their karma, how we react is ours."
-Unknown

To alchemize low vibrations in the heart, find light in the darkness. Think of everything from a place of love and not fear. When trauma comes, yes its perfectly okay to feel that shit, let it simmer, let the anger and the rage inside. But then, find the brighter side, figure out what u can gain in love from each situation. When we're swallowed in it, it's easier to be blinded by darkness; unable to see the light at the end of the tunnel. But if you look within, I promise it's there every single time. When you find it, you always find gratitude for that darkness bringing you closer to unconditional love. That is when your heart is gold. That's when you push past the surface of the earth and see the sunlight; allowing you to grow into the beautiful flower you were destined to be.

176

All in all, everyone walks a different walk and everyone deals with their trauma in a way that we may never understand; it's not for us to. I realized all the holding on to the people I resented and all the situations that brought me pain was making my heart heavy. My heart was completely guarded from letting love in and fully giving love out. I had to understand we are all souls on a difficult journey and unlock the unconditional love within my heart. This allowed me to forgive these gentle souls who were just acting in fear. I reached out to some as well forgave many in silence.

The hardest part of all was forgiving myself. I had to look at the little girl in me and forgive her for not knowing better at the time she was feeling hurt. I had to forgive her for letting others tear her apart and giving her power away. I forgave her for developing coping mechanisms and survival patterns. Little Tyler was who I needed her to be; she was strong, she kept going, she did what she had to do to protect herself. I had to understand my personality was only the traits I developed to deal with my shit. That wasn't really me; I didn't mean to hurt myself or others (same goes for other people). Then, I found peace. Sometimes the hardest thing to do it let go of the old version of yourself. I had to let go of the old Tyler; she served me well and brought me many incredible experiences and lessons. She fought so hard to get me here; I thanked and appreciated her so much.

After I forgave and moved tons of heavy emotions through me is when I felt lighter, in balance and harmony. When living life with an open heart, life seems more peaceful, our eyes adjust to the beauty we've been blinded from, and we finally open up a gateway to receive all the love we deserve. Although there was much more growth to do, I reached a point where I saw light.

Signs and Synchronicities

About half way into my awakening, I began to realize what was happening to me. The more I mediated, tapped into the spirit inside me, and I lived in the flow of things, the more peace I gained with my situation.

I felt so in tune with the universe; like I was a part of the effortless interconnectedness. There was an inner knowing; I was able to feel God, my angels, ancestors, and all spirits around me sending me signs to let me know I was in alignment. Let's just say my third eye was poppin; intuition on point. I received little bread crumbs reminding me to appreciate how much I've learned so far; but, to keep growing.

Synchronicities are repeating numbers, signs, and symbols we see to confirm things for us. The universe is made up of numbers; mathematics and geometry come from the cosmos. After all, everything adds up and aligns. Shapes in nature reflect geometry, like how the sun and moon are perfect geometric circles. Let's just say the universe would pass AP trig, calc, and finite with flying colors. So, whenever we see a sequence of numbers repeatedly, that is outside energies, those not of this physical world, communicating with us. Remember how we talked about the fact the human ear can only hear and the eye can only see a very small fraction of the frequencies all around us. Those extremely high frequencies everywhere are guiding us if we embrace ourselves as a spirit and not just a physical form. We can catch so many signs when let our spirit listen and observe. To do this we must raise our vibration in various ways and allow our chakras to open up. We can only see signs and synchronization when we raise our vibration and surrender to the oneness. All the answer we need for our own healing, our purpose, and any endeavor we face in life is within us.

Everyone is different and entitled to their own experience with universal signs. However, from my personal experience all energies surrounding me whether they be God, angels, or my ancestors, they communicate to me through numbers all day long. Certain numbers popped up in several places every single day; time, likes on Instagram, views on videos I watched, temperatures, and so many other things.

Not only are numbers signs, but also other energies which make up the universe. Music; certain lyrics happen to be exactly what I needed to hear at the time I was listening. Seeing certain animals or insects also convey messages from spirit. Animals all symbolize certain characteristics; we when see them it's a message to tap into to the energies of that animal or to show us we are flowing in those energies already. Messages were communicated to me through my dreams as well; things I was about to experience and lessons I needed to learn. For me, everything we encounter is a message from the universe, because not one thing happens without purpose. So, I pay attention to all the signs in and around me which are there to help further me along my journey. Think of synchronicities as the universe trying to get your attention.

The universe puts signs in front of us all day every day. Most of us aren't present enough to see the meaning or lesson behind them. We let our emotions control our response instead of taking a step back then evaluating and reacting appropriately. One time I found a hair in my chipotle, this also happened to be a time where the universe was trying to communicate a lesson involving my hair (crown chakra). Another time, a couple kids shattered my car windshield; at first I was highly aggravated, then I realized the universe was trying to help me by pointing out the fact that my perception (the looking glass in which I see life through) was being tainted by the people around me. If I would have stayed angry instead of being present I would have never saw what the universe was trying to help me with and probably would have dug myself into a deeper hole. The signs we receive won't always bring positive emotions, some may scare us or make us angry. What we have to constantly remind ourselves is, everything that happens is attempting to show us something.

The beautiful thing about signs and synchronicities is they remind us we are never alone. Despite the fact we cannot see them with our human eye, if we tap into our other senses, activate our spiritual essence, and open our hearts to receiving guidance, our spiritual guides, ancestors, angels, and all spirits of the universe water, fire, air, and earth will communicate with us in ways we understand the most. They are waiting for us to acknowledge them and receive the messages they are trying to send us. Be grateful for them. It's a beautiful thing to be guided through this entire journey, knowing we never walk alone.

External Cleansing

All of this cleaning of vibrations definitely had some side effects. Think of everything as energy and vibrations. According to Bruce Tainio, inventor of first frequency monitor, cold and flu begin at 50-60 MHz; aka, how fast or slow the vibrations within our body are.[1] All these low vibrations I held in finally came out into the physical; the last manifestation. So, because I was cleansing my inner world of low energy, all of that energy had to come out in the physical. I went through things like acne, sinus infections, and mucus build up; the list goes on. Yes, it was actually real life tragic. Although, it helped when I began to think of these as the physical form of all the shitty energy I had piled up inside finally breaking through. Then I was all "let that shit out!".

As I began to see the energy of my physical body change, other physical energies outside of me went through a cleanse as well. Many of my relationships began to fade away and my environment changed. Like my body, parts of my physical reality began literally purging and cleansing. I even tried to go back to some old realities, but they just didn't feel the same.

"If you want to fly, give up everything that weighs you down."

-Buddha | Monk

We must cleanse old energy to allow room for new manifestations coming in. In order to step into the new reality, the one I worked so hard to create for myself, I had to fully let go of everything no longer serving me; leaving old habits, old ways of thinking, and old ways of doing things behind. This wasn't all at once, it was like an onion, me constantly peeling off layers and old versions of myself. I purged old ways of eating and even down to my old skin care routine. I detoxed the hell out of my life. I'm talking deleting numbers, Facebook friends from 2010, cleaning out my closet, and deleting old photos. Even cutting off hair that no longer served me. Our hair is crown chakra; I wanted my hair to be full of divine energy not old ways and experiences.

Just like the trees let go of old leaves and flowers let go of petals, we wouldn't become new if we did not release the old. Don't be afraid of change; welcome it. Life is a constant redefining and shedding of layers. Nothing is permanent, not even our perspective. As we experience more lessons and pieces of our lives puzzle, we developed new ways of seeing and understanding this reality. So, if we change our minds, our opinions, our beliefs, our style, or everything about us, good, we're evolving. We are only ever rough drafts of ourselves, constantly making corrections. Our potential is infinite; so, just flow with it. Don't be defined by who you were last year, a week ago, or even yesterday. Continuously shed layers of yourself to become new.

"Just as a snake sheds its skin, we must shed our past over and over again."
- **Buddha | Monk**

Transformation

This was not deprivation; this was transformation. This was part of the process of restructuring and realigning every part of myself. My personality, attachments, identity, desires, and mindset. When we truly heal, we reprogram everything down to our DNA. We become connected with divine nature, our higher self, and carry a new vibration. When you let go of past trauma and open the heart, you change your vibration. When you change the vibration within yourself and the aura of light around you, everything no longer a match just vibrates the hell out. Allow all new love to pour in and reinvent your entire outer world.

Because everything fell apart I was able to put my pieces back together in a higher vibration of love. My truest self was released from being buried behind my ego, fears, belief systems, cultural conditioning, and unconscious self-sabotaging. I'm now able to continue freeing myself from any other self-protective personality traits I've developed to deal with trauma. I am now the butterfly; I am now the flower growing toward the sun. I can now see the light. My true spiritual energy has been unleashed; this fire energy has burned through low vibrations within me.

Leaving me with a glow incomparable to any highlighter on the market. A permanent glow from the deepest parts of me; a fire that cannot be extinguished. Pure sunlight. I entered the spiritual world. **#Naturalisthewaytoglow**

Tips

These are tips that help me throughout my awakening; take it or leave it. Remember, everyone is unique.

- Staying present
- Meditating daily
- Praying
- Burning sage and Palo Santo to cleanse energy
- Using crystals to tap into different frequencies
- Journaling
- Writing down dreams/dream interpretation
- Yoga
- Binaural beats and sound frequencies
- Singing bowls
- Uplifting/Meaningful music
- Isolation (embrace the solitude; the answers are inside of us)
- Reviewing personal astrology signs (Greek, Egyptian, Chinese, and Native American)
- Tarot readings
- Diffusing essential oils
- Limiting outside influence/ Creating boundaries (social media, Television, friends, family etc.)
- Spending time in nature
- Reflecting daily
- Detoxing
- Refraining from alcohol (escapism is not the key; a sober mind is a clear mind.)
- Connecting to people who are on the same path/ have been through an awakening.
- Never giving up.

Remember: Singing bowls, binaural beats, crystals, tarot, sage, and such are all tools to help us heal and tune into our divinity. But we must know we don't absolutely need these external remedies. They are just tools to assist us and strengthen the connection to the divine. We are all spiritual beings just as we are. We are the universe expressing itself. When we realize we need no external sources to heal and tap into our spiritual nature is when we are truly awakened and aligned.

Activity

Feel It All

Healing traumas, internal wounds, and shadow aspects of self is some of the hardest work you will ever do in life; but the most worth it.

1. Go back to what you wrote down in the previous activity and begin to feel those hurts again. Yes, this will bring up the same pains and wounds. Remember we have to feel, heal, and release; not suppress. This could take days, weeks, months, or years. Just start.
2. Write a hand written letter to any person(s) who has hurt you.
3. Pour it all out, leave out no details of how they made you feel.
4. Curse them out, call them a name, call them on their bullshit, but as you reach the end of the letter, find the light at the end of the tunnel.
5. Seal the letter in an envelope and keep as a reminder of your growth. Or, burn it. Do as you feel.
6. Write another letter to yourself, same directions apply.

Chapter 12
Balance

Spiritual World and Physical World

After my awakening I spent a lot of time in my spiritual chakras. I was exploring different aspects of my mind, creation, and the reason for our very existence. Getting to know my own energy and my spirit guides, while heavily meditating, visualizing, and manifesting. Basically, I spent a lot of time in my head; my own inner world. This was an incredibly enlightening phase; however, my root chakra became under active. I was a little too focused on the spiritual aspect of things; the invisible world. Forgetting, I am still in a physical body in a material world. I had to get back into how I take care of my physical body and my physical world. I began consistently filling my physical energy body with love again. Things like eating a balanced diet, taking the time to cater my hair needs, and spending time on my skin care, and keeping up a workout routine. Even small things like keeping my nails and toes tidy and putting effort into my appearance again. The things that I used to be overly obsessed with, I now forgot to do. I now understood it's okay to take care of ourselves, care about our appearance, and have nice things; that doesn't make us materialistic. It's all about the balance of showing ourselves love in our spiritual world and the physical one; not valuing one over the other. I also had to start connecting with my outside physical world again; I spent so much time in solitude while exploring my spiritual side I forgot what it's like to interact with real people. I had to remember to stay present instead of 24/7 daydreaming of my future manifestations unfolding. Although I love that about myself, it's healthy to balance all the head stuff with the actually real life stuff.

Ground Me

I feel like I'm flying

I feel the air on my face

I almost feel free

but I can't find my footing

the ground is so far away

I can't even say

I feel safe

I don't

I feel brave

like I'm taking every risk

taking every sip

of courage

where is my security?

 the reason I don't feel completely free is ...

I can't see

I can't see what's in front of me

I've been flying blind like a bee

is this how it's supposed to be?

when do my feet make prints in the soil?

when do I move past this inner turmoil? of me

experiencing anxiety

I'd say I'm on my tippy toes

trying to get around

Though, truth is...

 I'm nowhere close to the ground.

all I feel is wind

like everything still exist in

my imagination

but I can't see the physical,

the earth,

the pentacles.

I've been flying over everything

like an eagle spreading my wings

and that's the beautiful thing

I have a higher and broader perspective

so gratitude is what I give.

But I've been surviving on faith

with no will to chase

only allowing everything I need

to land right before me

as it all has

but now

And these few days that have passed

I feel lost

it's cloudy up here

And I'm starting to meet fear

as I continue to flap my wings

 I can't see a damn thing

 I feel like somethings ahead of me

or behind me

creeping up to swallow me

and take me a different route

Where it will let me out

into a new territory.

will be painful?

Will I feel glory?

I have no clue

this is where the fear comes into making me forget to breathe

and see the beauty

of the unknown

my comfort zone

is not where I belong

I want to keep moving along

passing each and every test

yet,

it's OK to lay my feet on the earth

and give my wings a rest

 that's when I fly the best.

Ground Me | Tyler A. Norman

Just as it was difficult to incorporate the physical world after my spiritual awakening it was just as hard to incorporate the spiritual world when in a physical mindset. After my much needed phase of solitude ended, I began going out again hanging around people and being exposed to the multitude of energies out in the world. I was having fun again and didn't have as much time in isolation as before. I had to learn to balance the spiritual lessons I had previously learned into this lifestyle. It's a lot easier to be peaceful, meditate, read, and dissect the mental and spiritual playground when there are no distractions; when the outside world is silent and almost nonexistent. But when there's chaos, noise, and distractions all around it takes serious discipline to listen to the whispers of the spirit. It's important to find solitude and practice spirituality yet also be out in the world experiencing real life.

There are times when we need to be submerged in the spiritual world because we need to hear the messages from the universe, learn our lessons, and be guided through them by our spirits and ancestors. Majority of the time I spent creating this book I was in complete isolation, because isolation was part of my purpose at the time, I needed it to go deep within my mind and spirit to express what I was called to. There are times when we are dancing in the earthly matter. Meaning our purpose at the time lies in connecting to the physical realm. When I later dove into teaching kindergarten I felt so disconnected with spirit at times because I was so used to being in isolation, feeling, and speaking to god within me. Truth is we are never disconnected; it just meant my purpose in the present moment was needed in the physical realm. Instead of connecting with my spirit guides all day it was a time for me to connect with the spirits around me in human form.

The key is whatever state we are in finding ways to still bring in a balance of the other side of the spectrum. So, I find myself balancing my lower chakras; those associated with the physical world, with my higher chakras; those associated with the spiritual world. Remembering I am like a plant; nourished by the sun and the earth.

"Our spiritual challenge is finding balance between the physical and spiritual. Living life fully and yet, being less attached to it."

-Unknown

Solitude and Social Time

Very similar to the importance of the spiritual and physical world is the balance of solitude and social time. This is pretty self-explanatory; we need time alone and we need time to engage with others.

Feminine and Masculine

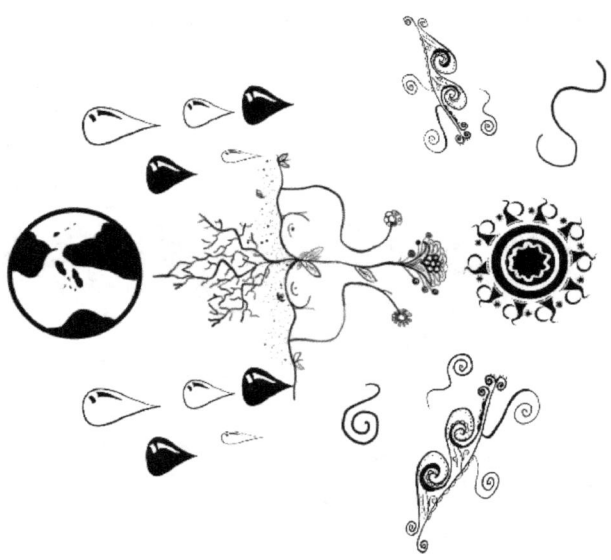

Feminine	Masculine
Yin	Yang
Night/Darkness	Day/Light
Physical body – Earth	Spiritual body – Fire/Sun
Emotional Body – Water	Mental body – Air/
Pisces, Cancer, Scorpio, Capricorn, Virgo, Taurus	Aries, Leo, Sagittarius, Aquarius, Gemini, Libra
Passive	Aggressive
Submissive/Codependent	Dominate
Nurturing	Protecting
Receiving/Attracting	Giving/Seeking
Intuitive	Logical
Emotional	Rational
Right Brain	Left brain
Curvy	Linear
Delicate/Soft	Strong/Rough
Beauty	Intellect
Protector in the spiritual realm	Protector in the physical realm
Attracted to mental energy and intelligence	Attracted to physical energy and beauty
Mother Earth's feminine energy births life into physical form of flowers, fruits, herbs, and all earthly plant life. She bears the seed in her womb until	The masculine energy of the sun provides light energy which gives nourishment to all life on earth. It provides light, warmth, safety, and guidance. The wind guides us,

it's ready to sprout into the outer world. She nourishes us. Water moves us, cleanses us, and all of nature.

How to embrace

Nourish the physical body by connecting with nature, getting the body moving, and feeding it with mother earth's energy. Nourish the emotional body by connecting with water and letting emotions flow. Dance, paint, sing, and tap into whatever forms of creation you enjoy. Embrace your sensuality and sexuality. Go with the flow. Trust your own intuition.

Tap into creative energy at night with the moon.

The moon is linked with feminine. Our feminine energy can be cleansed or recharged by the moon. The moon cycle has effects on the tide of the oceans; it deals with water. The moon also has effects on our physical body, which is made of 70% water and our emotional body, which corresponds with the element of water, both feminine energies. If you want to activate, renew, or cleanse your feminine energy take some time to connect with the moon; study the different phases and absorb its energy.

moves us, carries us, and cleanses us along with nature.

How to embrace

Nourish spiritual body with spiritual exploration and acting on your true passion. Nourish mental energy body with an environment conducive to your growth, reprogramming your mindset, and embracing the ability to change direction. Embrace your intelligence. Speak your mind. Create a routine. Trust your own personal power.

Induce productivity in the morning with the sun.

To recharge or reconnect with masculine energy we can spend some time in the sun. The sun is fire; masculine energy and spiritual. Our masculine energy deals with protection, leadership, being in command, and giving. The sun is the provider of light energy on earth; which gives life to all things. Spend time with the sun; let it recharge your spiritual body. Let yourself see the suns bright light; activating light in your mental energy body as well.

Chakras	Feminine or Masculine
Crown	Feminine and Masculine
Third Eye	Feminine
Throat	Masculine
Heart	Feminine and Masculine
Solar Plexus	Masculine
Sacral	Feminine

Root	Feminine and Masculine

Seasons	**Feminine or Masculine**
Spring	Feminine and Masculine
Summer	Masculine
Fall	Feminine and Masculine
Winter	Feminine

I linked up with a mutual friend one day and we had a super enlightening conversation about feminine and masculine energies. What those energies act or look like, the importance of each, and how we believe we should embrace them. At a point in the conversation I asked him, "what energy do you feel from me?" He went on explaining when he knew me by sight and few encounters he picked up a very feminine energy. But, after really getting deep into a conversation with me; he believed I was a more masculine energy. I was somewhat offended by this; I started to regurgitate ways I emulate femininity. I listed off my creativity, nurturing ability, secretly intense emotional side, and how I'm so wavy with the shits. It was like I was almost afraid to be masculine; it would somehow take away my femininity. I asked why he felt this way and he began listing the masculine qualities I had; my directness, leadership, analysis, independence, and boldness. All qualities I knew I had and was actually quite proud of. My own confusing contradiction to my personality is what drove me to begin studying the feminine and masculine energies.

In my world I tend to see a lot of overly masculine men afraid of femininity, a lot of feminine women looking for masculinity to make them whole, and a lot of masculinity disregarding feminine energy as equal to masculine. I held this idea that a male should be a representation of complete masculinity and females a complete manifestation of femininity. I was not aware feminine and masculine energy aren't even necessarily connected to female and male physical bodies; it's all energy. Although I think all female bodies possess feminine energy in some way and male bodies possess masculine, a male body can have a lot of feminine energy sometimes even more than masculine. Just like a female body can have a lot of masculine energy that sometimes extends the feminine. But, because of what I saw in my world I subconsciously separated the two energies; believing we were one or the other. When actually this inability to be fluid is toxicity.

Not only did I separate them, but like many I've been psychologically programmed to believe masculinity associated with men is superior to femininity. We live in a patriarchal society, society functions with men in superior roles. For example, look at all the white male presidents (shout out to Barrack Obama) and the fact that men still get payed more than women. Even through my former religion; it portrayed god as a masculine energy only. Although this god was never given a physical identity, the son of god is also a male figure, a white one at that. Meaning if anyone were to ever picture god in human form it would be a white male because *his sun* is white. Which in my eyes is only part of the whole system to encourage white male superiority (this is what I mean when I say religion is a reach for love polluted with human error). The gag is, masculine and feminine energy is what creates life as a whole. Not one being more significant than the other. Different, yes; but unequal, no. We've been given the wrong idea of the power and oneness of these energies. After this discovery, I had to learn to balance my energies inside me. The feminine and masculine are meant to be two in one; duality.

It may be easier or harder to tap into the feminine or masculine energy for every person at different times. Usually we naturally find it a bit easier to be in tune with one of them (at least in my case). I'm an Aries woman, the way I tackle life is from a very steadfast and driven standpoint; like a ram I always want to move forward and just go. How I think, process, and communicate information; how I take action and assert myself; my self-discipline and social life all function with Aries energy. If you're not into astrology, basically I'm always on 10. Much of my chart is fire and air;

masculine energy. Then, there's a little Pisces energy to make sure I'm not a complete explosion. Both feminine and masculine energy flow through me; I love tapping into my creativity and nurturing abilities plus my passion and intellect. Yet, my ego and the way I go about life are often functioning through masculine energy. Like I mentioned earlier, I had this idea of parts of feminine energy being weak. In order to bring in the balance, I had to put effort into letting more of my feminine energy in the mix. Naturally, I struggle with embracing my softer side; it's like some part of me whispers "man get off that weak shit" when I get emotional about something. Even though I'm low-key super sensitive deep down, I know I'm supposed to feel, heal, and release, and I completely understand the purpose of our emotional body. There's often a resistance I have to work a little harder to push through in order to activate feminine energy. The resistance is much stronger when my masculine energy is ignited by my own will.

There are many factors which can contribute to our feminine and masculine energy being lost in the sauce or turned toxic. The traditional teachings of society make it harder to embrace both energies. Picture having two children; only feeding and embracing one. Plus, having the disregarded child do the cooking and nurturing for the embraced. The one child that is embraced now has a big ass head and is being overfed causing it to developed toxic traits. Due to the child's upbringing it now believes it dominates over the other. The two children are the masculine and feminine energies; the children of the universe. We have been conditioned to embrace one child over the other; we're missing the balance and we must allow it to return. I believe part of the returning of world peace comes when we open our arms and welcome back our divine feminine nature which then allows us to return to our divine masculine nature as well. When we learn to balance power and love. Though many of our wounded feminine and masculine traits come from a variety of different traumas; we all need the same medicine; internal healing. We need to listen and heal the divine feminine and masculine within us, allowing us to activate our purpose, bring back harmony into our lives, and eventually the world around us.

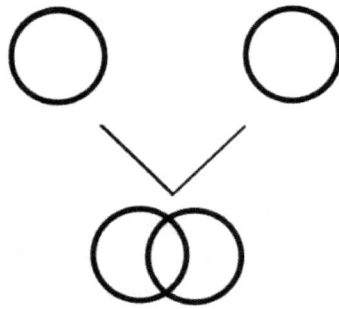

The way I see it, there's a universal father/masculine and mother/feminine energy that creates life. There's a father/masculine and mother/feminine being that comes together to create our life. And there's a father/masculine and mother/feminine figure inside of us. Think of our feminine and masculine energy as our inner mother and father of our inner child. So, the relationship we have with our inner child is identical to the relationships we have with our physical birth parents and whoever played a more feminine/motherly and masculine/fatherly role in our lives regardless of gender. What does your inner child need from you? Exactly what you needed your parents to be as a child, and now. To heal the inner feminine and masculine look to your parents as a complete mirror to you. Spend time with and appreciate your parents, they are here to serve as a mirror for us to identify what we need to alchemize in order to be the best person we can possibly be. That's a gift. If you don't really mess with your parents remember any behavior you find bothersome from them is triggering the wounds you need to heal in you. If you need help figuring out and having compassion for them, spend time with you grandparents; understand the energy which developed your parents. If you don't know your parents and have no way of getting to know them. You can still study the whatever feminine and masculine role model has brought you up as a child; brothers and sisters, aunts and uncles, or family that blood couldn't make any closer, as influence of behavior is still a contributing factor to who we are.

Signs of wounded feminine energy

- Repressing one's truth
- Unworthiness
- Lack of boundaries
- Codependence
- Depression
- Passiveness

Signs of wounded masculine energy

- Overworking
- Impulsiveness
- Anxiety
- Aggression
- Controlling
- Emotionless
- Dictating

Once we begin healing and channeling both energies, we can learn balance. Balancing both, embracing both, and being whole instead of boxed into categories based off characteristics; limiting who we are. When we operate in a state of one energy by itself, without the balance of the other we are only performing at half of our full potential. A healthy human being should carry a both feminine and masculine side; not be afraid, ashamed, or overpowered by the other. We are meant to be fluid; both energies are equally beautiful and have needed qualities for a sustainable well-being of any life. Once we draw in the energies of both, the challenge becomes learning when to emit whichever characteristics align with those energies.

If I were to recollect the puzzle of my life, there have been several phases where I am solely absorbing and emitting the energies of the black or white side of the yin yang. I'm either super hard working to the point of overworking myself in strive for perfection or praying for procrastination to pass me by. After reaching a place of enlightenment I finally started recognizing the pattern. The lesson is always balance. When I have masculine energy on overdrive where I'm overworking myself, bossing people around, making quick decisions, giving to much of my energy out, and spending much time in the external world; the lessons I learn all equate to being patient, peaceful, and taking time for isolation; pulling back in my feminine energy. The times when my feminine energy is poppin where I'm staying up late at night, with no structure to my day. Just creating in all forms; painting, drawing, dancing, cooking etc. the challenge is to create order and mix in a schedule. There was a period of my life I experienced different events, people, places, books, and dreams; all small pieces to a larger lesson. After enduring, reflecting, and placing the puzzle pieces together, I saw similarities in all the different daily journal reflections. All of these various experiences I encountered were all steps leading me to healing and activating my divine feminine energy while my masculine energy was taking the lead. Then, learning to heal my divine masculine bringing it in balance with my feminine.

When I say balance I don't mean 50/50; I mean keeping the energies alive and well within us. That way, when we need one we can express it. For example, we need both energies within us to maintain financial abundance or any form of abundance. The masculine energy is the giving; the hard work, the determination, and the drive. The feminine energy is the receiving; the openness which attract fruits from the seeds you've planted and tended. Both of which create a circulation, a flow, and infinite source, aka abundance. We need feminine and masculine energy to run a successful business. We need the creative, unique, and attractive component and the logical, orderly, and determined component. We need both to be any form of an artist; feminine energy to help creativity flow within, yet masculine energy to express those creations and share them with the world. We need the masculine energy to put out our manifestations and the feminine to receive them. All in all, we need contrast and fluidity of feminine and masculine in all endeavors through life. Maintaining both allows both sides of the coin to coincide within and allows us to always have the energy and qualities within that make us whole; a complete being and the true manifestations of God we are.

After this lesson I understood and loved myself on a much deeper level. I am divine feminine energy manifested on this earth. I echo a feminine spirit by the way I create, connect with mother nature, feel, and my display of beauty. But don't get it twisted I will never be afraid to express my masculine traits I been gifted with; I will protect myself with my masculine energy. I am hard on outside and soft on the inside; like candy. We can be beautiful and smart, delicate and strong, intuitive and logical, or nurturing and protective. Tap into all these amazing traits we have within us to create the oneness of an entire universe inside us. Then once we learn to balance both we unlock the door to our inner child, which lies in the heart, the center, the balance.

Together feminine and masculine are life.

The Moon

Being of light

There's been So many moments spent experiencing you

You keep me up at night,

it's something about your peace,

your patients, and softness.

The way your energy exchanges with my wild fire

It's like that perfect time of day

Where it's not too hot, not to cold,

the suns setting and day and night start to Blend in.

You balance me,

make me at peace internally.

I know you're only reflecting my own peace,

yet your presence magnifies it.

Your presence brings with it the feminine energy

which is random

And has no order,

Creative, curvy, water in motion

I surrender

I surrender to the love

I surrender to the fear

Because

You reflect in me

the darkness I try to hide

You show it

Clear in front of me

Where I can't ignore it

I can no longer put my umbrella up

Logically moving

avoiding emotion

It's you who shows me

The dual natural of all reality

Everything we see

Is light and dark

Curvy and linear

Up and down

Equal opposites creating oneness

You show me the importance of healing and wholeness

The way you openly gift the world with a new view of yourself each night

Making me appreciate you in your entirety

Though you go through these phases

you remind me how everything is truly connected.

The Moon | Tyler A. Norman

Ego and Soul

Ego is I, me, myself; often the part of us that finds home in our comfort zone, compares ourselves to others, looks to compete, and seeks to be filled from the outside. Soul is us, we, one; the part of us that desires growth, focuses on our own soul path, serves others, connects with God, and seeks to fill our inner world with love.

A deep lesson I had to experience showed me just how much I was functioning with my ego. For a long time, actually my whole life, I was all about me, myself, and I. I had this serious ass need for independence. I wanted to do everything on my own, work for myself, and earn everything in my life by my damn self. It's like it made me feel more powerful, hardworking, and deserving if I succeeded without any assistance. If I were to create a movie I would want to be the writer, director, producer, camera gal, actor, costume designer, makeup artist, and editor of the whole thing. That's just how intense it was. Being able to claim I did it with no help really boosted my ego. But it only felt good until I actually started feeling like I was doing everything alone. What once was making me feel more powerful was starting to drain me and leave me out of breath. Unconscious of my own behavior, I wondered and asked why I always have to do everything alone. Why am I so alone in general? Then, I started seeing I manifested this reality by pushing everyone away who tried to help me and being so determined to do things on my own. The lesson was for me to feel this emptiness, stress, and lack of energy that comes with trying to play every role. I encountered roadblocks to show me I actually can't do it all on my own and I was never meant to. The role we play and the work we do in this life is not just about us, it's bigger than us. Our role is intertwined in a collection of gifts, passions, and purposes of the entire collective consciousness. We're meant to build on, play off, and connect with other great minds with our same vision. Not one person creates a multimillion dollar business all alone. Not one person makes this world go round by themselves. Not one person is responsible for raising the vibration of this planet. It's a collective effort which is why our souls desire to connect.

We're supposed to put our talents, our stories, and purposes together. Two is stronger than one. Three passionate energies are stronger than two. Four dope ideas can combine and turn out better than the original.

What I had to understand and what I'm trying to get across is, teamwork is actually what makes the dream work. We know there is no I in team. There are others souls who we are meant to connect with to co-create businesses, projects, families, homes, or anything we truly want to enact our purpose and impact the world. It's not I, it's we. I am not here to change the world, we are. Ego is about power while soul is about love. This lesson allowed me to step out of my ego so much and ask for help from the physical reality around me. I also realized, not only did I need connection in this physical world but the spiritual world too. I had to go through a period where it seemed like the spiritual world, spirits in nature, my guides, ancestors, and angels, weren't guiding me as loudly. For me to see just how much guidance I am gifted with daily. They say absence makes the heart grow, I had to be absent from people in the physical world and the spiritual world just to remind me how much I needed both. We are co-creators with the universe, the source, and oneness of all divine spirits. We never have and never will do this on our own. Show gratitude for the help and gifts of connection we receive from the both the spiritual and physical world instead of pushing them away.

Practice knowing the difference between what feeds your soul and what feeds your ego. A good way to find out what struggles our egos face is to look at our sun sign; our zodiac sign tells us different shadow sides we carry with us. My Aries ego has a deep desire to be independent, a leader, and always be number one; my soul has a desire to connect and serve others love. I can balance out both energies by still being an entrepreneur and working to support myself, but also remembering no successful business is ran solo. I balance power, love, and wisdom; therefore, I can still cater to my ego but also my soul.

The ego seeks fulfillment from material things; we can still ball out at the mall and buy ourselves nice luxury things but with a balance of the soul. Knowing these things don't complete us or define us and are only temporary. We can turn up with gang, off Henny and coke but know these altered states of mind are not our only euphoria. Know we can't escape but we can engage. The point is not to try and silence our ego but to balance it. Were here for a good time. We are all humans still; our ego is what keeps us human. Without it, we would never learn the hard lessons we need to further develop our soul's purpose.

It's important to love ourselves for the god/goddess within for all of our amazing and beautiful qualities. It's also important to love our human form, the part of us that messes up and will continue to. The human form of us that is sometimes run by our ego primarily, we have to love it too. Though we should love ourselves entirely in spite of any egotistical flaws we may have, we have to take responsibility for our shadow side too. Which means we must work on our bad habits but realize we're still human. Welcome, accept, love, and be one with your shadow. Introduce yourself, and let it to you. Let your shadow be present without judgment and allow it to teach you and bring you closer to pure love. Recognize your shadow for how it is just as much a part of your growth and evolution as your light. Give gratitude. We can still love ourselves unconditionally where we are at while still working to heal and grow. That's self-love; balancing the ego and soul.

Chakras

Chakras can also play a role in balancing ego and soul. When your chakras are open the ego and soul are finding a balance; when they are underactive or overactive one is weighing heavier than the other. To find a set of open chakras we must access all trauma, programming, and conditioning causing us to portray certain personality traits associated with under or overactive chakras. Which means we must go through spiritual healing so we can understand both our ego and our soul. Before having my spiritual awakening my heart chakra was underactive while my root and throat were through the roof; everything was out of balance. After opening my heart chakra which is the harmony between the spiritual and physical chakras, balancing all of them became easier.

Chakra alignment takes deep internal healing; healing often done in layers. However, there are so many little ways we can help keep our chakras cleansed and open. We can wear colors associated with the chakra we need opened, eat plant foods that correlate with those colors, use essential oils associated with those plants, and even connect with the frequency of crystals which match that chakra (placing them near the energy point). Along with using the vibrations of crystals, we can listen to certain sound frequencies and musical notes that match the energy of the chakras. All of these outside sources aid in the opening of under and over active chakras; but, like all things the real work is done within. Chakra work is endless; there's still so much I have not even scratched the surface of regarding them. With that being said, I encourage you to do your own research on activating these magical energy points within us.

Chakras	Underactive	Open	Overactive
Crown (Purple) Spirituality, knowing, and connecting. B note	Close minded, rigid, unaware of spiritual world, depression, lack of faith.	Connection and oneness with all of the universe, faith, wisdom, awareness.	Obsession with spiritual world, lack of physical self-care, ungrounded.
Third Eye (Indigo) Intuition and Seeing. A note	Heavily relying on authority figures and belief systems for answers. Incapable decision making.	Use of intuition, listening to gut feeling, relying on self for answers, healthy imagination.	Head in the clouds, fantasy driven, living in own imagination, and experiencing hallucinations.
Throat (Blue) Communication. G note	Inability to speak mind, stand up for self, and express one's truth.	Ability to speak truth, express self, speak up for self, and great communication skills.	Speaking when unnecessary, oversharing, gossipy, and lack of listening.
Heart (Green) Loving, relationships with self, and others. F note	Resentful, unforgiving, distant, guarded, and lack of empathy.	Harmonious, unconditional love for self and others, compassion, kindness, and balance.	Overly giving, putting others before self, drowning others with love, and codependence.
Solar Plexus (Yellow) Doing, accepting, and personal power. E note	Low self-esteem, unaware of own strength, and lack of confidence in self.	Confident, knows own strength, acceptance of self, driven, and powerful.	Domineering, cockiness, critical, competitive, and power hungry.
Sacral (Orange) Feeling and creating. D Note	Fear of intimacy, stiff, shame of sexuality, lack of creativity, emotionless, and closed off.	Sacred sexuality, sensuality, openness, affection, closeness, healthy flow of emotions, and creative energy.	Very sex driven, overly emotional, attachment, and manipulative.
Root (Red) Grounding and stability. C note	Fearful, out of place, running from situations, unsafe, unwelcome, and feeling of being in the wrong place.	Grounded, safe, present, centered, care for physical body and physical world, security, and feeling of being at home.	Stagnant, obsessed with material world, hoarding, obsessed with safety, greedy, cynical.

Talents

It's so important to cater to all of our gifts and talents; every last one has a piece in our giant life puzzle. All of our talents are a part of our purpose. It's time to start embracing them all. We are multifaceted beings; we have more than one characteristic that makes us special and many ways to express ourselves. So why put all our biscuits in one pot. There's no reason we should have to fit in a box of understanding or a specific title. I love acting on all of my gifts because I get to be every part of myself. I get to paint for a few days, then travel, do some writing in between, teach a class, and then pose for some photo shoots one day. This may be my Gemini moon showing with the fact that I desire to multitask and be involved in a ton of things at once. But, I do it so I don't get bored with just being one thing. We are infinite beings. I choose to explore as much of it as I can. Open all of the gifts around you; it will feed your soul. #Naturalisthewaytoglow

Work, Rest, and Play

Not every day has to be a work day. Not every day is meant to hustle, be booked, and busy; busy doesn't mean successful. Some days are meant for reflection, brainstorming, and configuring new parts of our story. Some days everything is just telling us to rest; rest our mind, body, and spirit. In order to truly put in meaningful and long lasting work we must take those days as is. We cannot give all we need to from an empty vessel within. Some days are meant for recharging and refilling our own vessel so we can unconditionally give out the love we need to in our work. Take those days; even if they're in the middle of the week; even if they last a week.

Not only are those rest days important, but playtime is just as relevant. I'm willing to admit, after I did some intense soul searching, I lived life way too seriously. My life was all about meditating for large amounts of time, spending time in nature hugging trees, going to the gym, and eating kale salads while I worked my ass off toward my goals. Yes, I'm very proud of how disciplined I was; but, I needed to loosen up. Life is not all about work, work, work. It's not even about work and rest. Playtime is essential to enjoying this journey. It's so important for us to find time to do the things we love, spend time with people we love, and just have fun. One day I was scrolling through my snapchat memories reminiscing on how incredibly fun my college experience was. I was a wild child; constant partying, making new friends, late nights, and experimenting different ways to turn up. I've always been the type to be down for whatever; I just wanted to create fun lasting memories. Although my past experiences differ from my ways of having fun now, seeing my old self still taught me something. Old Ty was all about adventure and I still can be; it's all about balance.

My message to you right now is to go play. Never let work take over your life so much you find yourself lacking moments of fun and adventure. Be free and let money flow into your life effortlessly; money is energy. It's not about reaching the destination; it's about enjoying the journey. We're not meant to work our lives away in order to survive. We get to work for our dreams yet enjoy life too.

Discipline and Surrender

The balance of discipline and surrender is very similar to the work, rest and play balance. In life we must be disciplined enough to make the decisions which further our growth. We need self-discipline to get enough work done, to eat right, to stay active, to study, and fight off the influence of negative thoughts and self-destructive behaviors all around us. We need a certain amount of discipline within us to move forward. Yet, moving forward also comes with surrendering; relinquishing our control over the course of events in our life over to the universe. This takes trust and understanding; we don't have control over all things. We have control over ourselves only; which is where self-discipline comes into play. Controlling the desires and behaviors of self; which in turn will have effect on the events in life. Yet surrendering, trusting, and letting the universe control the rest. The balance of discipline and surrender is what creates flow. Hustle and flow baby.

Elements | Energy Bodies

We should have this down like clockwork by now.

We are an extension of God love high frequency energy; we are a soul. Our soul is the driver of a vehicle made up of these elements which we create a reality of human life on earth.

Fire is what gives us that push we need; fierce and fiery energy needed to fulfill the desires of the spirit. It's what connects us to our masculine energy and what gives us a longing for true creative will and passion. Fire also helps us be sexual beings. This connection with spiritual energy fills our life with sunlight. Connect with the sun and light candles.

Earth is what gives us stability; the ability to stay present in our roots and grow where we are planted. The energy that allows us to nourish our bodies in every way and focus on what's in the now. From the earth comes all of our fruit, veggies, and herbs. The earth is the nutrient source of the trees which provide us oxygen. We need to stay grounded in Mother Earth by not only what we consume within our bodies but in the outside world as well; garden or dig your feet in the mud. This energy transfer is powerful.

Water is what allows us to let emotions flow in life. To connect with our feminine energy of water instead of piling up emotions like rocks making us heavy. Those rocks which will sink us to the bottom of the ocean. Keeping our emotional energy healthy is the ability to stay afloat instead of drown in life. To allow creativity, softness, and adaptability to flow through our being. We need water to cleanse us internally and externally, Mother Nature cleanses the earth with rain. We are made of 70% water in our bodies, were connected to all the large bodies of water which make up 70% of the earth. Take a bath, visit the ocean, or cry.

Air, our atmosphere, is what lets us be open and free. It's the wind that allows us to be blown in different directions. What allows us to be open in our mental space and absorb all the knowledge and beauty around us. Also, what makes our mental energy thrive. Accepting change in our perception and not settling down in one frame of mind. Allowing the wind to move us freely from one perspective to the next; true growth. Take some deep breathes and open your mind.

Light and Dark

This is probably the most important part of the book I want you to remember. Sort of like balancing ego and soul within ourselves, we must balance light and dark; in our inner world and outer world. Life is not perfect; instead it is a journey where we constantly fuck up, miss chances, take leaps, live freely, and learn lessons to help us love a little more unconditionally every day. In this journey, we are never fully healed, we are never all light, and we are never perfect. It can take a whole lifetime to heal a certain trauma and release the baggage we carry. Those bags might come back over and over and new bags will be added on. This is a nonstop healing and learning journey. There will be tough day's full of anxiety attacks or days we slip into depression. There will be dark periods of our lives that change us completely. There will times we are scared of what's next, where we have no idea what the hell we're doing. Some days we'll stick to our routine and others we'll wake up at two in the afternoon. Some days we will absolutely love the shit out ourselves; some days we'll find it hard to. Then, there will be amazing days where we experience the greatest adventures and find ourselves filled with joy. There will be moments we are full internal happiness and find ourselves completely submerged by love in every way. Moments we thought we could never experience and people we never thought we would meet will enter our lives. What we need to accept is all of these moments are equally as beautiful. Amazing moments and tough times will always come around because that is the balance of light and darkness within the universe. This is the cycle of life. Find peace in knowing every pain and every pleasure has purpose.

"A beautiful thing is never perfect."

- Ancient Proverb

Everything in the universe abides by the law of duality; the sun brightens our day and can also burn. The rain cleanses and provides the earth with nourishment but also floods. Every form of creation has a light and dark energy; us, everyone else, and everything else. We must remove the idea one side is better than the other when each side makes everything whole. We need contrast. Life is all about the balance between high and low vibrations, dark and light. Because it's the yin and the yang; the wholeness. We need fear to learn love, sometimes we need to eat a low vibrating food to remember how much our body thrives on high. When I fast it makes me appreciate food on such a deeper level. It has me thinking about the different flavors of each herb and truly being grateful for the experience down to the details. When we're away from people we love it makes us cherish the moments together so much more. When it's been a hot summer we begin looking forward to the fall. Then, when the cold hits we developed appreciation for the spring. We need pain to heal. If everything was one side of the yin yang all the time, there would be no cycle, no growth, no rebirth. We wouldn't have the four seasons. We'd have to pick between day and night. We would become comfortable and accustomed to what's in our reality and lose the appreciation and love toward it. We need the low moments to appreciate the highs. We need our shadows to teach us and our mistakes to help us grow. It's not about being all light and love all the time, it's about balance. Accepting our darkness as beauty yet alchemizing it to light.

For a while I chased this perfect version of myself, I wanted to be completely free of chemicals, low vibes, and any pain. When in reality, no matter how in tune with our spirit we are, know that perfection is just not possible. We are humans and humans make errors; over and over again. That's what life is; constant learning of lessons meant to bring us more wisdom, love, and purpose. We will never have everything figured out and we were never supposed to. So let's let go of the expectation of ourselves, others, or anything in the universe ever reaching perfection. Let's just be real. Healing and inspiring others starts with letting people see vulnerability. Sharing how our life is so imperfect rather than pristine at all times. The more we see how we are all a balance of light and dark the more we can learn healing, connection, and love.

Find your own balance between what low and high vibrations you allow in your physical, mental, spiritual, and emotional body. Find what experiences will align you with your destined path in this lifetime. Through this learning experience called life we are just here to learn. Though it may take us years to find it in ourselves and others, ultimately this journey will lead to unconditional love and that's what's important, that's what's worth it, and that's what keeps us going. We are here to constantly reflect, heal, and commit to loving ourselves and others every single day.

"You won't always be up. You won't always be down. Life is a medley of high and low notes. Just sing your song the best that you can."

- **Unknown**

After understanding life as a real experience and not a perfect one, I now hold a perspective where I see a lesson for growth in every situation; a chance to continue turning every darkness I may face into light. This perspective gives me a constant state of gratitude and love for myself and others as I understand everything is always growing and evolving. We must love ourselves through everything that shows up and just flow with life; be in the moment. We were meant to be lost, found, renewed, and lost again; which makes our story that much more dope. Have some fun and just live. Life's perfect imperfection is what makes it real and beautiful.

Everyday

What I've learned after opening my chakras and continuing to reach enlightenment is, balance is everything. Life is about balancing different energies within us so we can reach eternal wholeness, happiness, health, and purpose; then, attract those things to us. It took lessons I'm super grateful for to show me how quickly our energy can be changed. For a while, I focused on carrying a really aligned set of chakras and made it my intention of keeping them that way. Then, the holidays rolled around and huge wave of energy came my way. I won't get too into it; but, long story short, working retail during the holidays can really fuck up your chakras. From this lesson I learned, in a matter of seconds our energy can change from the energy of foods, colors, people, sounds and EVERYTHING around. We go through so many different seasons of feeling different ways. So it's not just one season of healing and that's all it takes. Its everyday; constantly reflecting and growing through this learning experience. Now, I continue the daily practice of not only balancing my chakras but everything that makes me, me. The balance of everything is what puts us in a place of peace and alignment. It's what opens the harmonious vibrations of our heart chakra which then shine out from our inner to outer world.

Past | Present | Future

The magic sequence of 3,6,9, the past, present ,and future all happening at the same time. Your unhealed past self, your elevated future self, and your current self are all existing at once, in you, in another life, dimension , and/or season. Sometimes we may need to be triggered by the past to go back and gain deeper wisdom needed to unlock something in the present moment that will lead us to our destined futured. Sometimes we need to see our future to get clarity on things we need to clean up in the present moment that we have carried from our past. Balance doesn't mean being in all of these spaces equally, the important thing is owning all of these beings within us, not getting stuck and living in the past, or in the future but flowing through each existence when, as, and if necessary in order to find our way back to the present moment. The present moment is the balance, the love, the source, and the magic.

Chapter 13
Soul Guidance

Physical Identity

I spent most of my life trying to be someone I wasn't. Trying to fit into a category so I could feel as though I belonged. Growing up, I bounced back and forth between public and private school. Providing me with two completely different environments and types of people. As a child trying to understand my identity and develop my character, the back and forth had me confused. Who was I? I became a classic case of too white for the black kids to black for the white kids. But, like I said, I didn't like that middle man shit. So I found myself wearing certain clothes, speaking a certain way, straightening my hair, and making myself physically sick trying to mold myself into a different body type just to fit in with one side. I never felt like I belonged anywhere. I never felt enough. My hair wasn't straight enough to be white but my hair wasn't kinky enough to be fully black. I didn't talk white enough but I didn't talk black enough either. I wasn't skinny enough and I wasn't thick enough. I was too mad because of my resting bitch face and I was too scared because I refused to throw hands over petty arguments. After searching for belonging in others for so long; I completely lost myself. I didn't know who I was. I questioned my ethnicity, my culture, my personality, my creativity, and felt as if I was just wrong in so many ways. All because I didn't fully belong anywhere. I based my identity off the conditioned ideas and behaviors of certain groups of people. Not knowing, I am the only one who creates my identity.

When I began loving fashion and dressing up at a young age I was told I trying to get attention from men. Due to the mature feminine swag I was dripping in, adults sexualized me when really I was a child expressing my creativity. Simply trying be myself. Grown ass motherfuckers had side conversations and group sessions about me wanting to get attention too much. For a while I went into depression and didn't dress up at all. I stopped wearing makeup, jewelry, and fancy clothes because I didn't want to be seen as thirsty for drawing attention to my beauty. I didn't want to give off the wrong impression or ruffle any feathers. I began wearing hoodies and sweats to cover up my body because I was so tired of being sexualized my entire life for having hips and breast. As a woman of color in the world, a lack of physical femininity was something that kept me safe many times. Safe from judgmental adults, other jealous women, and disrespectful men who think cat calling is identical to having game. Every time I tried to be myself I got shot down for it; so I found it hard to understand who I was. Somebody was always trying to tell me about myself.

I once dreamed of a choking baby, the baby got something caught in its throat and couldn't breathe because the air way was blocked. I performed the infant Heimlich Maneuver on the baby but my arms were weak. I turned the baby over and saw the outline of its heart coming through its chest as if it was so strained and blocked it could no longer pump blood through the body. Suddenly the baby was fine and a family of 3 enter the room. A mother, father and daughter. The daughter was showing me her new outfit and how cute it was. But she said sarcastically and disappointingly, "my dad made me get extra extra-large pants just so men won't look at me with perverted thoughts". I thought, wow why are you so strict and controlling of your child? Why are you labeling your child this way? Your preventing her from fully expressing herself and living freely, your teaching her to be concerned with how others may view her. I reached to hug the girl and simultaneously her father called her over to sit. She quickly hugged me and went. She was now in trouble for speaking on her annoyance of her father's ego. She cried. Her mother sat there quietly, hands shaking, as if she was upset but couldn't say a thing about it. As if the masculine had an unhealthy control over the expression of the mother and child. The mother was my inner feminine energy, the father my inner masculine, and the little girl my inner child. The choking heart failing baby was my blocked throat chakra (expression) and heart chakra (how we give and receive love). I've had been over protecting and holding back my inner child expressing itself through what I wear, what I do, and how I love

226

people. All because I'm assuming my inner child will be sexualized or misunderstood. Remember earlier in love languages I mentioned I often hold back my giving love language of physical touch? All because it's misconceived too often. I had been holding back how my inner child wants to express itself through my fashion and how I want to love people. What I've learned from this dream is, our inner child only wants to be free. It has no worries about who's looking or judging. Truth is, we can't control anyone's reaction to us. The reactions we fear and expect from people is what we attract and we will continue to attract these reactions to trigger us until we heal the wound and let our inner child live.

When I did embrace my physical appearance I still didn't quite understand true self-love and beauty quite yet. I tried to be beautiful in the eyes of the world. Like most young girls I followed society and associated beauty with a certain standard; a standard that continuously changes every decade. The thing is, we can't keep chasing a moving target of beauty standards; it if it keeps moving and changing, the chase never stops. The longer we keep running toward an idea of beauty, the further we run from the real definition. Chasing a standard means us running away from ourselves; dimming our own beauty. We destroy ourselves physically, mentally, and financially during the process. Standards have us desiring the same hair, clothing, eyebrows, and attitude. Pretty soon we will all look, act, and think the same. There's nothing beautiful about a society with a lack of uniqueness. Why pay to cover up our own features to match the features of someone else or an ideal image? Why be afraid of people seeing the real us; our real hair, our skin, our body, and our voice? We don't have to belong or fit in to any ideal standard to love who we are. An important thing I've learned is there is no solid definition or standard of beauty; there an idea which has been conditioned in our minds. There's no ugly either. There's attraction, either we are or aren't attracted to something or someone. We're energy remember, what were attracted to has to do with our own selves, it doesn't define someone else.

I am not defined by my curly hair, I am not my trauma, I am not defined by the way I speak. I don't have to belong in a category of the way I should dress, act, speak, or who I should kick it with. Our spirit is our guide to who we really are deep deep down. Our spirit doesn't box us into categories based on our physical vibration. Our physical form is a complete manifestation of our spirit. Which means, we are literally exactly who we are supposed to be. We gain nothing by trying to change it, were only furthering ourselves from our soul's guidance. It was time for me to stop conforming to the issues of society. It was temporary comfort and acceptance or self-expression and growth; you can probably guess what I chose. I've learned and still am learning to completely fall in love with every aspect of my physical form and not only that but embrace it and share it with the world. I love my hair because it's mine; so I'm going to let my hair be free. I love my beautiful brown skin; so, I'm going to show it. I love the way I speak; so, I'm going to express myself. I love my curvy and sensual body because it is what my spirit has gifted me with. I will not be ashamed of or hide anything that forms me.

I realized I can be sexy; my sexuality is power. It's the powerful energy that creates life. Through my sexual energy a soul can be channeled from the universe into this very earth. That is a magical creative energy; it's life force energy running through me. I don't have to cover up everything because some people might treat me like prey. Me wearing a bikini is not shameful; me wearing a crop top is not me asking to be flirted with or touched. It's me embracing my body; being free and living at loud. I will no longer silence the life within.

Dear Fashion,

My true love,

though my love for you is unconditional and our journey has been long

it's been a rocky.

Different phases I experience effect how I tap into you.

Often you've been my means of self-expression

 creativity displayed on my physical essence.

Yet also a way I've used to conform to society;

using "trends" just to fit in.

But either way I express you

whether it's from my authentic self or my people pleasing self.

There's a flip side to you ,

you've been an energy which awakens the green eyed monster

Something that when I'm heavily involved in I receive more side eyes

for longer

It seems

The way pieces of you hug my curves;

giving them attention

reminding those parts of myself are love and not shame

seems to evoke sexualization...

and not in the spiritual nature it's meant to be.

unspoken and spoken thoughts make their way to me...

I feel it in their energy

"who is she dressed up for?"

"She dresses because she wants attention from men".

My inner world plastered in plain sight.

Their treatin me like my love for you is a sin

giving the world a glimpse of my dopeness before I even open my lips.

Judgment appears.

Sneak diss,

Is it worth all this?

You are a yin and yang,

a blessing and a lesson....

so we've been rocky.

At times I forget about you;

letting my desire to create thru you slip thru my fingers

because ur darkness can be heavy...

at times I'm head over heels for you.

Steady

Screaming my artistic genius through your Wave of color

This time,

this phase,

I've done my inner work,

I've searched

Within

I've detach from my outer world, my appearance,

and I've gotten to know myself without you.

This new found energy I've dug up inside me

 Of authenticity

 creative expression,

and not giving a single fuck about who's looking at or judging me

This lesson

has brought me back to you;

stronger.

The thing about unconditional love is..

no matter how many ups and down or darkness's that may come with this love...

whether we leave or we stay

We end up wiser

Letting those dark moments allow us to rise up

loving it harder than the last.

Deeper than the last.

Fashion, I've decided to love you without limits or conditions

Without rules

Or attention

To the fear in the eyes of those who I don't even need to mention

Dear Fashion | Tyler A. Norman

Spiritual Identity

During my spiritual awakening I started making some pretty huge ife changing decisions. The direction my life was going prior did not suit me. Things I consumed myself with were not feeding my soul. I was fo low ng a safe path; a path that was drawn out for me not by me. Some of these changes were huge; dropping out of college, starting self-education, stepping out of my previous religion, and becoming plant based. Some were smaller; changing my style, cutting my hair, and not shaving my legs for a period of time. Regardless of significance all of these changes were something very foreign to those around me. I was seen as eccentric a hippie, or just someone who was lost in life and needed to find their way back to reality. People assumed I was going through a life crisis: typ cal for a girl in her twenties.

For a long time, I was extremely sensitive to the opinions around me. I started to feel so lost and misunderstand in the mist of things. It hurt me my life choices were something others highly disagreed with. I hated others couldn't and didn't even desire to understand my perspective I spent spend so much time and energy trying to explain myself to eve yone. Trying to seek validation and feeding my approval addiction. I hated others didn't believe in me like I believed in myself. I wanted everyone to see the wisdom behind my choices, the strength behind my mindset, and the magic hidden in my spirit. I spent nights in tears; wanting so bad to be understood and to be agreed with.

"You are here to understand yourself, not to be understood."

-Unknown

Once I became okay with not conforming to normality, I still needed some sort of community I could relate to. I just wanted to find people I could fully express my spirit around. Once I did found a group I could relate to, there was a pressure to be quote on quote spiritual in the eyes of society. It's often a misconception to be spiritual or a free spirt indigo we have to do yoga, wear white flowy clothes and flower crowns, want to live in the woods, and walk around barefoot with hairy armpits. I tried to fit into this category with the rest of the world who called themselves spiritual; it wasn't working for me. I had to sacrifice parts of my true desires to belong in that category of people. I just wanted to be a hundred percent all of me; not playing a part. When I followed a crowd there was always something I had to lose about myself. When I followed my own spirit, I lost the crowd; but, I found something much more valuable. I found authenticity; when she showed up I realized fuck these categories fuck these boxes I don't fit into. I'm a little bit boho, a little hippie, a little artsy, a little boujie, and a little hood. Not defined by one box because I can't be contained; I will not be contained. I am fully and authentically myself. Every decision I made after was completely my own spiritual guidance. I am not here to conform; I am here to create a new wave. My own wave.

I finally felt like I was myself again. Very slowly but surely I finally started to embrace every part of myself. Not needing to be understood, or around others who were like me, but truly expressing my own spiritual identity.

Authenticity

This is my life; I create my own reality. This is my soul inside this body and in this life; no one else. Who am I to let everyone else draw out my life for me. My soul has already done that, and it is my guide toward all things in alignment with my path. I didn't come here to be a puppet. There is no right way, there's my way. Being truly tapped in doesn't have a ook, its doing whatever the hell your soul tells you. Not thinking you have to subscribe to mainstream bullshit; But truly doing you and not worrying about anyone else. I'm just me; you're just you. No need to have a name for the way we are; we have actual names. We're not a category we along with everything else are creative expressions of the universe. We are art, we are us; exactly who we are supposed to be.

"Consciousness has no religion, no belief or ideology, no gender, no sexuality, no race, no age, and no nationality. You are consciousness."

- **Unknown**

With authenticity, I learned to completely embrace my physical and spiritual identity in the ways I desire. Our most authentic self is a balance of our highest self and our shadow. So, I can twerk all night at the club, take some shots, and come home to meditate. I can wear what I want; flowy clothes to my ankles, booty shorts, crop tops, or be naked. I can believe in what I want; cling to whatever religion I vibe with, not claim any, or claim them all. I can be who I want. I have the power to choose whether I wear my face beat to the gods or no makeup at all. I decide if I want to come through drippin in Gucci or shop at the thrift store. I decide if maybe I'll shave my legs or let them be. Maybe I'll eat a plant based diet then smash some crab legs if I feel like it. I choose what music I listen to; I can vibe with Jhenè, bump to Pac, Cole, lil baby, YG, and Nip, then throw that ass back to some 21 Savage too. I may just combine all of these things because life is about balance. I choose what people I surround myself with and I choose every detail of my life. I may choose difficult lessons but at the end of the day I am always pure unconditional love; guided by my own spirit.

Trust your inner guidance; trust your journey. Life is so much better when you're not trying every way to be something you're not. So, do whatever YOU love to do; go be a stripper, do some modeling, make art, chef it up in the kitchen, make music, be a fucking librarian, start a business, or write a book. As long as you are happy and filled with unconditional love, you're winning. Don't let anyone tell you shit about it.

Live Out Loud

I once had a dream I was in my house and someone was trying to break in. I was terrified. They broke in successfully and let a ton of people in my home; my safe space. The guy that broke in started hosting an open house in my house. No one was hurting me, everyone was just looking around inspired and curious. I wanted to take off and run. Our home in a dream represents our inner world. I realized then, I've always had this fear of letting anyone into my inner world; allowing others to see the real me. Each new way we learn to express our truth, whether it be through what we say, what we do, what we wear, or what we make, it takes strength. Our internal energy is out in the open which gives people the opportunity to admire, be inspired, jealous, or treat us like prey. Which is why it takes strength for us to open a whole new layer of vulnerability to the world. This opening does set our inner world on display, but most importantly it opens us up to receive more love no matter how scary it may be.

If I wanted to grow I had to let it all go; I had to see vulnerability is absolute power and strength. Me writing these very words is me letting go; I am setting my inner world out on display like an open house. I am constantly reminding myself I can live out loud and not be afraid to share my truest self with world. So, my advice to you is, don't go out and live life afraid; be open and free. Live; go on adventures, fall in love, then cut. Speak your truth, display your work, and share the fruits of your labor. Let the world see your magic; your creations, your gifts, your prospective, and your style. The world needs it all; otherwise you wouldn't be here. When we hold ourselves back and filter ourselves, we are preventing the universe from expressing itself. We're blocking energy which is meant to be and flow. So, take up as much space as your energy can expand, dim your light for no one. Even if others are judgmental, threaten, insecure, or intimidated by your presence, don't let that stop your light from shining. We have no control of others reaction to us, it's based on their own perspective of reality. So, we might as well enjoy being our most authentic self out loud.

Don't let the fear of dying, failing, being broke, being heartbroken, or lonely stop us from living out loud. Anything we are constantly fearing we are only attracting; what we vibrate we attract. Remember we are air, were supposed to flow whatever direction life takes us. Any resistance to life comes out of fear. When we live life in fear, we miss cut on opportunities, growth, and all the beauty in everything that surrounds us. With the lowest frequency constantly vibrating through our being we cannot live in love. Fear no longer has power when we face it. Each fear we come face to face with; a new level of love and freedom we gain.

Living out loud is connecting with our spirit and inner child then releasing it; but, also opening ourselves up to connect with others on the outside. Guidance from our soul will allow us to be vulnerable, free, and open. This openness will automatically inspire others to match this vibration and attract others which we can share our authenticity with. When we free ourselves we give others permission to be free too. Living out loud and letting in soul connections is what allows us all to be free. We must bond with other souls which are here to help us live in our purpose.

Living freely is to experience and connect with all types of people from different upbringings, cultures, and practices; embracing and loving all those around us. Different people open up neurological pathways in our brains that can be lit up in no other way but through them; because their uniqueness and creative depth to their mind and soul is completely unique. Once we eliminate the expectations we've been conditioned with, we'll realize there's no specific age, race, gender, or number which is right. When souls have a genuine connection, it's always right. We should let our brains be fully enlightened by connection. Set boundaries but connect.

If you choose to only surround yourself with people who look, act, and think like you, or avoid connections all together, you are living in your comfort zone. We know by now; a comfort zone is a place where growth doesn't exist. The more we connect with the multitude of mirrors which make up the universe, the more we realize we are more alike than different. The more we will see ourselves in others and understand we are one.

Be Thyself

Everything aligns; nothing in the cosmos useless. Everything and everyone plays an important piece of the entire collective puzzle. No one in the universe is just like you and that is your strength. Own your puzzle piece and the world can be a beautiful picture.

When you begin to wake up you start to understand everything as a whole in a more open minded view instead of conforming to the beliefs and behaviors you have developed. Realizing everything is infinite there is no certain answer that's absolute truth; everything is perspective. The answers or truths in our current awareness are just our perspective at this certain level of consciousness and energy vibration. Everyone sees life through a different pairs of eyes. So, of course our perspectives are all different. Those set of eyes we look at the world through were perfectly crafted for us; meaning all of our own perspectives are technically true because they are ours. Our soul guidance is the only foundation we have for any truth; so we must follow it. We also have to realize no one's perspective is the same; everyone's truth is different which is why we must accept other perspectives as they are. Share your perspective; but at the same time agree to disagree instead of forcing someone to look at life through your own specially crafted pair of eyes. Just like when you switch glasses with people; you can't see shit completely clear because it's not your prescription. Where your own damn glasses, but realize your prescription isn't the only way to a clear vision.

I go with my truths; the answers my soul is gives me at any given time. Not being limit to an absolute truth allows us to freely change our perspective as we grow. We have to know ourselves, understand the whispers inside of us, and begin to let the fire of our souls lead the way. Anything that gives us a fire or spark within our spiritual energy is a message from the soul. I think our passions are really just feelings of our highest self being activated because it's remembering what we sign up for before we came. When we do something we truly are passionate about it's like we feel a freeness that makes us want to fly. Well guess what, we were born to fly. When we do things we truly love doing our soul is letting us get a taste of what it feels like to truly be our highest self. Listen to whatever makes you feel most alive, what gives you drive, what makes you feel like a purposeful human being, and follow whatever reveals a fearless badass version of you. **#Naturalisthewaytoglow**

Get to know your soul and let it guide you to the life of your dreams...

Chapter 14
Biggie No Smalls

Pathway to Success

There's so much pressure on us to go the way right way or the safe way. Basically everyone wants to tell us what to do and how to do it. Graduate high school, attend a credible university, go to grad school, get a high paying/high title job, and work until you retire. The painful truth is, there is no right way. We are energies that create our reality by what we think. Our mental energy creates the experiences we have. The reason we think we have to go to college and get a certain job to reach success is because we been told so; our mind has been conditioned to believe this is the way to success. We've also been programmed to think other things like what foods taste good, what products work on everything, and what's the new trend through Tell-a-Vision programs and advertising. That's beside the point; our mind can create whatever it believes it can, whatever it's been told it can create. This is all one big ass lucid dream if you ask me. In lucid dreams the mind can realize it's in a dream state and begin controlling the narrative of the dream. The only difference is, that is dream state and this is awake state. Regardless, in both states of consciousness we are projecting an illusion of reality and we can control our end of the narrative; were co-creators with the universe.

Unplug

Imagine being in a video game; your mind is the controller and your body is the video game character. Whatever the controller communicates to the character, the character will do. If the controller wants to change the settings or background; the background changes. What the controller does; the character and setting does. Who or what is holding your controller? Who's guiding the concepts in your mind that control your reality? Keep your soul your controller; or you'll be living in a video game system. Next time you make a decision ask yourself how did I come to this conclusion? Did I hear this from someone or be told this is what I should do? Or did it completely come up from within me?

Follow your own guidance and unplug. It's scary as hell trust me; when I decided to stray from the typical pathway to success, it felt like I fell off a cliff. I thought I was going the right way; I was about to be a junior in college excellent grades, multiple internships, involved in the school's recruitment organization, Vice President of a mentor organization, plus other campus involvement. I was bound to be successful when I got out of college; I had titles; according to the game system I was aligned with success. Yet, at the time I still felt lost. I wasn't full inside and I wasn't in alignment with my true self because I wasn't following my dreams. I always knew I wanted live life big, but right then I was playing scared; following a map that wasn't made for me. Also, a map that does not guarantee success. According to U.S Census Bureau, there are 3.6 million bachelor's degree graduates who are still living in poverty; despite that degree![15] While some of the richest and most successful business people in the world are college dropouts. Overall, what I've learned from my years of fixed education is we pretty much pay for training to work for other people. We're taught the information needed not to go after our dreams but to work for companies to further their dreams. Making them far richer while thinking we are making a subpar salary.

When really we're being confined, limited, and living small while aiding in the big economic growth of the oppressor. When we retire that's it. There's no businesses, artwork, ownership, legacy, or no capital left behind for our family. All the energy of ambition, creativity, and dedication we put out is being limited when returning to us.; its blocked. That's not what we came here for, we want to cycle energy of abundance to our offspring.

If your own pathway to success involves a systematic and formal education, great; go to school. For me, attending a university had many pros as well. I was exposed to people outside of the box I grew up in, I saw hard work and success from people just like me, and I was able to build a network across the world. But if your pathway doesn't involve attending college, don't feel pressured to; everyone's path is unique to our life's purpose. Do what works for you. Luckily, I figured it out early a fixed education was no longer for me. The education I was receiving didn't seem useful to me; it was not in the speed nor direction I needed to go.

However, I learned no matter what the path, we all need some form of education; knowledge is wealth and knowledge is infinite. So, I began self-education; also known as auto didacticism, the collection of education without the formal direction of institutions. I choose what, when, where, and how long I study information. This can be through multiple forms; reading books, watching documentaries, going to conventions, or just observing the world around. I fed my own self the knowledge I was seeking instead of being fed specific knowledge I was told I needed to know. I took myself to various workshops, seminars, conferences, and certification courses to hear other perspectives and build up my knowledge in desired areas. There are endless ways to collect knowledge; self-education is putting our own development in our hands.

In the same time range I would've been dreadfully pushing through my junior year, stressed over exams, and trying to keep my GPA afloat, I instead wrote my first book, created, and began building a career as an entrepreneur. Experiences that brought me closer to my goals than ever before. Though I still have a tremendous amount of learning to do; learning that never stops, I took the leap of faith and it was worth it. I followed my own destiny. **#Naturalisthewaytoglow**

Faith Over Fear

We find it easy to put our faith in everything outside of us; pilots flying the plane or CEO's of businesses. Why do we find it so hard to have faith in our own inner universe? If we want to live out our destiny, we must trust. The only thing that will allow us to take our own pathway to success is faith. Faith is the light that shines through the tunnel when we have no idea yet which direction to go. Putting faith over fear is how we make it happen; how we decide to keep going. To truly follow our divine path our faith has to be imperishable; no teacher, parent, friend, or anyone can say anything to make us question ourselves and our journey. I would be lying if I said there wouldn't be times when doubt creeps in and we aren't too confident in our inner guidance. But even a small inkling of faith keeps the tunnel lit enough for us to keep heading toward the light. What's important is we let those moments of doubt pass over us and never let our fear outweigh our faith.

Intention

"Whether you think you can or you think you can't, your right either way."

-Henry Ford | Captain of Industry

This quote spoke to me on a deep level when I first came across it. It was a boost to my faith knowing when I set my energy accordingly; everything will turn out in my favor. Maybe not exactly how I planned or expected it to, most likely not even at the time I wanted it to; but, intention never fails. After recognizing the power of intention I began setting them for my entire day. Every morning, freshly rolled out of bed I started my day off with a meditation and prayer. In the midst of my prayers I set my intentions for the day; today is going to be a beautiful day, today I am going to have peace, today I am going to attract new opportunities, and today I am going to walk in my divine path toward greatness in all I do.

Previously, I mentioned when we pray we are speaking to God; we are sending out a frequency into the universe. When we meditate we are listening and gathering answers and guidance. I discovered my prayers were me sending out an energy/intention out into the universe prior to whatever I was going to do. After I implemented this intention setting and praying into my morning mediation time, I realized my days pretty much went how I set them out to go. Anything believed and set in our minds, body, spirit, and emotions; will come out how we intend. Energy is powerful.

What we believe we can do and what we deserve is all we can do and receive. Our beliefs have an effect on our overall energy field; creating certain vibrations within us. If we believe we don't deserve the life we dream of or we are unworthy of something, we are blocking that energy from ourselves. We cannot align with a vibration which does not exist in us.

Whatever you believe you can do and set your efforts toward is what will happen. Not what we desire to have and do or what we keep saying we'll do, it's what whatever reality we expect and believe in deep down within us is the reality we manifest. So, set a real intention before everything you do. Set an intention of doing all things with love and you will never be wrong. Love means blessing, miracles, and more love coming to you always.

Manifestation

Throughout our journey to success what if we all carry our own personal magic genie to grant whatever we wish? What if his genie is infinite, there is no wish it cannot accept, and nothing is too small nor too large? What would you ask for? One dollar or one billion? One vacation or free trips for life? This magic genie is the universe; the same universe that birthed the sun, moon, and stars. The one that creates the human body.

The one that keeps the earth magically floating in the middle of darkness. The same universe where the sun rises every morning where no mistakes are made. That magical genie is real. What are you asking for? One dollar or one million dollars? Use the universe to attract abundant riches into your life.

Though It's often a misconception money is the root of all evil, it's not the money which causes forms of low vibrating energy; it's the fear inside the person handling the money. Money only makes us more of what we already are. For example, if you're a racist; money is going to have you funding racist organizations. If you're materialistic; money is going to make you obsessed with buying objects. It's a circulation of energy; give and receive. The energy we put into it is the energy which is circulating, giving you clean or dirty money. So, if you are a free spirit of love, money will allow you to experience life at a higher level of freedom. More travel, bigger business plans, more giving, and more peace of mind. Plus, the ability to ball out and treat yaself in whatever ways you desire. Stay humble, give gratitude, share your abundance, and continue collecting your coins, gathering your fruit, getting this bread or whatever y'all want to call it. Be open to receive and give and you are in flow. I believe abundance is our natural state; the universe itself has an endless supply of everything it needs, meaning naturally so do we. We deserve unlimited gifts all throughout our lives and we can have it if we tap in. What we call money is only a measurement of abundance, just like inches, feet, and Hz are measurements. Therefore, if we are in alignment with the universe this measurement should be unlimited to us.

There is a whole universe in and around us; we are magic genies capable of creating our entire reality. We create whatever we allow our mental to believe we can; what we think we can't have is only a limitation create by our minds. Remove these limits and we will see we manifest everything into our lives consciously and subconsciously. We have the ability to choose what illusion we project. Each thought form we have opens up a whole new parallel universe in itself. Since we create this

246

illusion of reality within our mind, every time we think a thought we open up an entirely new illusion in which the reality we live is divinely foreordained.

"Every belief you have creates a portal for the corresponding parallel reality to manifest."
-   **Unknown**

There are millions of different realities we can choose to create. God Universe can change the reality we live in but it's all up to us first. The universe waits for us to change our inner world before it follows suite and creates a different illusion in our outer world. Our spirit, ancestors, angels and all light is what is guiding us toward making decisions, opening new neurological pathways, and feeling emotions that will create the reality we most desire. Why play small when we can play large? Why create a mediocre life when we can create an exceptional one? Why think smalls when we can think biggie? Think big, exciting, and loving thoughts and we will create a reality based on those. Don't limit yourself; we are unlimited.

We have the power to bring our biggest dreams into our reality through manifestation along with visualization which go hand and hand. To do this we have to believe we already possess the future we desire; it's already ours. See yourself there, think about all the big things you want to do day and night. Imagine it in vivid detail; see it visually and beginning to create an experience with all of your senses. How will all of your senses feel? What will you be smelling, tasting, seeing, hearing, and touching. Associate an emotion with how you will be feeling, then start feeling that emotion. Get clear on exactly what you want. These types of visualizations are magic; they activate the powers of the genie we call the universe. What we continuously visualize we are creating in our reality. Life is an open canvas; create a masterpiece.

"Though is powerful in all phases. Even in my career, even in my life, things end up exactly how I visualized them."
-Nipsey Hussle | Rapper, Entrepreneur, Father, Legend

Detachment

When I first starting building my own pathway to success I was thirsty with a capital T. I was direct messaging every Instagram page I could to give me a shout out. I was desperately trying to gain followers; I even sent all my blogs to well-known people in hopes I would get discovered. My ass sent my work to Mr. and Mrs. Obama's Dms; I'm not even joking. I had just started and was trying to get big overnight. If you ask any successful person, they will tell you sustainable success takes time. We must create a foundation which takes constant rebuilding, reediting, and critiquing. To fully align with our manifestations, we must take time to master our craft. Which means, be open to reworking and developing instead of rushing and ruining our work.

"Nature does not hurry yet everything is accomplished"

- Lao Tzu | Philosopher, Writer

When creating your dream life there's a thin line between over striving and acting when necessary. Action is a vital component of making dreams reality; but also letting things come. We are required to chase our passion and all things which are for us will chase us at the right time. What's meant for us will come with ease because we attracted them. When we are striving toward something and it seems like everything keeps getting in the way, it is our spirit, ancestors, guides, and the whole universe protecting us from walking the wrong path. Its divine intervention. If we are in alignment with these high vibrations, our subconscious can also manifest blockages which are meant to steer us in the right direction. Trust those blockages and continue manifesting your desired reality; you'll get there. However, if we are not yet in alignment without our highest self, if we are full of fear and low expectations, or if we have yet to recognize our power, we must assess and remove the conditioning which is subconsciously creating blockages from our divine path.

"If the door doesn't open, it's not your door."
- **Unknown**

It's not about the chasing or the striving. It's about accepting and just fully being present on the journey. When we focus on reaching destinations, once we accomplish what we've worked on we may get that high feeling of yes I finally did it, but it won't last long. Soon enough we will be on to chasing the next accomplishment. Then, life will become about running to the finish line and chasing the destination. We'll have a lack of presence and be throwing off our work, rest, and play balance. Our ego will be weighing heavy and we'll lose sight of the fact our time here is about enjoying the journey of life. Stop focusing on the future so much because we have no idea how things are going to play out. We need to experience the moments that are right here right now. Take the opportunities to look around at the beauty and lessons of life.

As you can probably guess, the only reason I'm able to relay this message is because I've lived through it myself. My Aries ass tends to try and fly through things full force. I even tried to rush the process of writing this book. I wanted to finish the book so bad, be done writing it, because it was such a long and tiring process. But I realized I had been striving toward a destination when there wasn't one. This book process doesn't end after I finish the last touches, see my first physical copy, sell my first book, or my millionth. There's no end. There was no point where I officially started writing it, every experience of my life has been building on this story. Even the experiences of the people before me. Therefore, There's no beginning. Experiences before my awareness of the book helped build the story, but also experiences while writing it. When I was rushing toward a peak and an ending I missed out on enjoying the journey of becoming an author. I did not acknowledge or even see how beautiful this whole ride really was. The process of writing this book, though at times long and draining, helped me grow into the woman I've always dreamed of. I found myself through my own expression and wrote my reality into existence. It was all in the process of learning and reflecting on lessons, writing chapters, and drawing sketches where I truly grew. Through it all I learned it's not that we reach a peak of growth, it's that we are always growing. We're always driving on this long road of life and when we only focus on making it to the end we miss observations, details, and experiences which serve a purpose for our enjoyment and the culmination of any work. This book taught me how to have patience and cruise through the journey because nothing created with quality is ever rushed. Trust me when I say, divine timing is perfect timing.

The universe is not in a rush, you are. This is not a race. Nothing's early or late. There's no timeline or time limit. All 7 something billion people can't follow the exact same path. Our schedule is designed for our own destiny. When we constantly worry and strive toward our desired destinations, fear of what's ahead is taking over instead of staying present in our currently reality which enables us to manifest our dream future.

Everything flows as it should, when working in our careers and fulfil ing our purposes throughout life we must remember that.

We'll know our manifestations are coming close to forming in the physical world when we are at peace and have gratitude for the present. When we are no longer striving and wishing the future was here. When we fully surrender to divine timing, when we relax, and find ourselves at peace with knowing no matter when our manifestations come through everything is perfectly aligned. We have to detach from the idea of controlling everything because truth is, we can manifest all we desire but we have no clue how or when these desires will manifest. The why, when, where, and how things are going to manifest is for spirit to handle. Simply believe your manifestations are already real because we've created them. We just have to do the work to align with them in due time.

Do meditations, visualizations, affirmations, and small actions like creating your logo for that business you want to start, opening up a tab for that book you want to write, fill out a deposit slip for that check you're trying to collect. Start the process but attract everything to you. Then, keep the energy you attracted not only alive, but growing. It will grow just as we do, in a cycle. The key to success in business and career is to allow the cycle to flow. Failure + redefine + reset + success, then all over again. Our manifestation are like our little babies, create them into existence and keep them alive and growing.

Do it For the Self

We live in a generation of flex, meaning a lot of us are out here making every move for the gram, the vine, the book, or the city; aka approval, liking, respect, and acceptance of others. We just want to show everybody what we can do better than the next, what we can buy, and create this idea that our lives are on point. That's why you've got people who post every single achievement of theirs on Facebook for the world to see. I do believe there is a such thing as sharing the joys in one's life for social reasons and also to inspire followers, but a lot of us publicize possessions and abilities to boast. Even small accomplishments like brushing one's teeth in the morning, "look at me everyone I brushed my teeth today, I gave a dollar to a homeless man, I have no makeup on today." Only to live in the comment section waiting to others to tell us how great we are. Whatever is it, many of us struggle with the desire to have things and succeed only for the flex.

Truth is, no manifestation of success last if we don't do it for the right reasons. So it's important to take a look at why we do the things we do. Why do we want to achieve the things we do? Is it to make our parents proud? Is it to draw in the attention of a significant other? It is to shit on everyone who doubted us? I used to want success so badly it's all I thought about. It's like I had to prove it to myself first and then to others I was capable of success. So I chased it; I wanted to always do instead of be. It became so overpowering I slipped into depression from thinking I wasn't reaching anything in life fast enough and feeling like I wasn't doing enough compared to others at least. Eventually I understood the idea if we truly believe we are meant to be successful there's no need to run around doing everything to try to prove it to others. Being booked and busy. It's just knowing; knowing our destiny and our purpose. Knowing what we do daily is enough. Without the chasing it's so much easier to be in the moment and enjoy the journey. Don't let ego weigh heavier than spirit and passion; manifest your dream life because you want to fulfill your purpose not just boss up on bitches or step on necks. Yea, it's cool to boss up but the intention is everything; we have to want to boss us, for the purpose of unconditional love, for ourselves first, and then to inspire others. When we do it for any other reasons things will always seem to be in the way, not good enough, or not fast enough.

The thing is, life is not a competition. So don't do things with the intention of outshining others, competing, or showing off for the gram, the book, or whatever city you rep. Do it for the self, with the intention to inspire others along the way.

Self-Mastery

I once went to a convention and one of the entrepreneur speakers said something that stuck with me, "jobs are like an adult day care." He mentioned, at a job you have to be told what to do and when to do it; that's what makes it so easy to conform with. However, if you want to create your own dream life, we must be capable of telling our own self what to do and when to do it. This was when I learned the importance of self-mastery. We have to maintain a high level of self-discipline to wake up when we need to, work when we need to, take leaps, and make the decisions we need to without letting fear get in our way. It's like putting our self in charge of steering the ship; we must master the steering wheel. Be in control of our desires, habits, and life. We have to master our inner world before we create the outer world we desire.

After this lesson I began building a daily schedule aligned with the life I wanted to live. I worked on maintaining a healthy sleep schedule, setting up time to create daily, and putting myself in situations for growth in every aspect. Self-mastery is creating a life of love toward growing our mind, body, spirit, and career etc. By our self; for our self. Just like I mentioned early in in balancing discipline and surrender. Self-discipline is a major key to success in any area of life. We need it to eat right, to find our purpose, to create, to wake up and pretty much make every next move. It's what determines our path. Though are path is dependent on our self-mastery, self-love, faith, manifestations, and intention, we must also trust the universe on its side of co-creation.

Activity

Make your Dreams come True

"Throw your dreams into space like a kite, and you do not know what it will bring back: a new life, a new friend, a new love, a new country."
-Anais Nin | Essayist

1. Imagine your dream life, write it down in as much detail as possible. Truly imagine yourself there and use present tense I am.
2. Have you figure out your purpose yet? If so, add in how you will walk in your purpose while living your dream life.
3. Record yourself saying your visualization out loud.
4. Read your visualization.
5. Listen to your visualization every day while working out, meditating, and even sleeping.
6. Program a new reality into your consciousness.

Chapter 15
Trust Divine Timing

Every Phase is What It Should Be

When actively growing and chasing our dreams it is inevitable we will face moments of despair. Moments where we'll be thinking "what the hell is happening to me?" We will have moments where we face a huge trial, where everything seems confusing, and things seem like they shouldn't be going in this direction. Low vibrations will start to cling onto the mind; thoughts of doubt and uncertainty of the future. Understand this, what is happening is preparing us for what we asked for. Everything is meant to be, everything happening is preparation for our next level. When we manifest a dream, the bigger it is the more responsibility and hardships it comes with. We must be prepared for all it takes live in the reality we have chosen. What good comes out of creating our dream life if we can't keep it going? We need to push through what we're going through, so when we get there we can keep it running.

For example, if a sports team is going to play in a national championship, they practice. They practice back to back until they master the skills they need in order to perform well when the championship comes. Practice can be gruesome; many times we can lose our breath, pull a muscle, and lose focus. But when the championship finally comes we will understand why all that practice and skill mastering was necessary; it's for us to succeed. This is the same with life; we must be prepared for the intensity of our dreams. We are being prepared for the dream life we asked for. We are mastering our minds, our lives, and our skills in order to maintain the extreme abundance and responsibility that comes with the dream we manifested. God promises peace not the absence of pressure; without pressure we would never have diamonds. Without fire, we would never have gold. When it seems like life is punishing you and your being constantly tested, know that you're just being prepared for everything you asked for. Life is a school remember, don't you want a study guide or pop quiz before your exam? Don't you want to be prepared? Think of it this way and you see the blessings in experiences and trials which only prepare us. Have gratitude.

Long Time Coming

When everything seems like it's taking so long, understand the universe is doing so much work in the background we can't even see. Arranging people, environments, and huge opportunities that match the vibration of the life we have manifested. The bigger the dream the longer it takes; the more things that need to be aligned and arranged. Trust; enjoy where you are and have faith things will arrive in divine timing exactly as they should. We are not capable of arranging everything on our own, some things are bigger than us. Luckily, God is on our side. The universe makes no mistakes and listens to our prayers and manifestations, let it do its work. Relax, enjoy the journey, keep your thoughts in alignment, and focus on mastering the skills needed to make the most out of your dream life. You have to be patient. Divine timing is a universal law. Plus, Nipsey told us, this shit is not a race, it's more like a marathon.

Look back on past scenarios and situations that have led us to where we are. Everything adds up, connects, and makes sense; well, that is when we take the time to put our puzzle pieces together. The universe is a powerful consciousness that created us, the complex brain, the human body, nature, the stars, and the entire universe as a whole. Who are we not to trust the reason for our very existence. Everything in the galaxy, the body, the mind, is perfectly piece together how it should be. There are no missing parts, nothing is ever late or missed placed, and everything is perfectly intertwined. The same goes with our lives; we are part of the universe and the universe is a part of us. We are a part of that alignment and interconnectedness to everything. Trust it, become one with it, and let it guide you. The universe is aligning everything for us and our faith will give it so much more love and energy. It will present us with the right people, places, and situations in divine timing. All we have to do is have faith, do our work, and wait for those opportunities to come our way. Then, we will use them to further guide us toward our divine assignment. As long as we are in alignment with ourselves, the universe makes everything happen at the perfect time.

There's a certain peace I've gained from understanding everything is exactly how it's supposed to be. Everywhere I go I'm meant to be, everything happening to me has reason, and every day goes entirely as it should. Even the small inconveniences; traffic, being late to work, or plans being cancelled. I've learned to relax; and remind myself, it's meant to be. With this wisdom; there is absolutely nothing to ever worry about. This brings another level of freedom into my existence; free from stress, worry, or questioning of life's circumstances. Just live and learn.

Move with the Seasons

Flow with the universal timing of life; like a mirror we coincide with the seasons. Just like nature changes and evolves, so do we. It's so much easier to understand universal timing when we flow with it. Summer time brings an abundance of fruit, vibrancy, and beauty in the outer world. Fall brings time of letting go of old leaves, harvesting, and pruning for increased growth. Winter brings a death of an old self, times for planting new seeds, nourishing the roots again, and going within the inner world for hibernation. Spring time kicks off new beginnings, a rebirth, new growth, and blossoming plants. Then, all over again.

In correlation with our lives there are times meant for us to grow and bloom to reach our full potential. Then, times we shed parts of our old self and begin to lose petals and branches that no longer align with us. There's a time we begin tending to the roots of ourselves, our raw and bare selves with no fruits. Then, every single time we begin sprouting into a new flower, that grows and fully blooms all over again. Just like nature; every life form, whether person, place, business, or a relationship must follow the cycle. We will constantly die and be reborn again.

Nature shows us the cycle of life and death; it's just a part of reality. I have this theory, though all of us don't physically die during the cold months, along with nature we still die every winter and become new again; spiritually. We must see the beauty in death of situations and old parts of us, unafraid of time or endings when everything is perfectly aligned and always has been. When we become enlightened, we'll see beauty and embrace any form of death just as much as we do life.

Love yourself right where you are, be patient with yourself, enjoy the process, learn the lessons, and know nothing is permanent. The next season will ALWAYS come. Don't be frustrated and fight the waiting period, use it as an opportunity to look within and grow. So when it's time for all the fruit to sprout again; we'll be ready. Be the flower; be the tree.

Life Goes in Cycles

Think of the world as the flower as well; with chakras. The entire universe goes through cycles as one just like we do in our personal lives. We must be buried in its root chakra, face darkness, then rise up, and burst through the heart chakra to reach full enlightenment. Our world goes through this same cycle; we as a collective move with it. What we experience is a paradigm shift; a shift in our consciousness as we move through the cycle. As the frequency of our mother earth changes during her glow up cycle, the frequency of our DNA changes with her, as we are her children and earth correlates with our physical bodies. We all instinctively vibrate on a wave which matches the universes and we develop new ways of thinking and living life based on that frequency.

Instead of shifting every season like nature, these paradigm shifts happen less often. According to NASA, The cycle of precession, aka how long it takes earths rotational axis to change orientation, takes around 26,000 years to complete.[2] The earth must move through 12 star constellations which are the 12 zodiac signs we know of (we also have 12 total signs in our personal charts). Therefore, we enter a new zodiac constellation roughly every 2,160 years in which the energies of the particular zodiac effect the consciousness of the planet. During these shifts a new world awakens as a new consciousness is reached. The cycle is infinite; as a collective we slowly rise up the chakras and experience an awakening. Then, eventually we fall and go through the process all over again and again; just like the flower, just like the tree. As a collective meaning we don't simultaneously all begin to awaken or fall asleep, but we slowly initiate the process because of the changes in our DNA and guidance of souls sent here whose purpose is to lead the collect ve into enlightenment.

THE FLOWER OF LIFE

Just like in our individual lives, we as one collective energy must fall apart, collapse, dissolve, and reach roots down in hell in order to alchemize, coagulate, ascend and bring darkness to light. Darkness is part of life's cycle and duality. Everything that rises must fall, everything that falls will rise again. This is the law of cycles and all life in the universe aligns. If you ever find yourself wondering why you're going through such a hard time or why is there so much evil and darkness in the world, in our countries, states, cities, and neighborhoods it is because we as a collective consciousness must go through the cycle. The system must fall to rise again. We must be separated, fighting war, and experience total chaos to finally reach a state of world peace.

I've learned not to be fearful or overly upset about the tragedies striking the planet each day. All I can do is act in my purpose of bringing needed light to the world and surrender to the cycle. Thankfully we are dawning the age of Aquarius. Meaning, a new world is rising; people are

262

transmuting and waking up out of the matrix. We are leaving separation, structure, systems, and order; we are entering a time of freeness, openness, and oneness. We can already see it. For baby boomers and generation X, buckling down, getting married, buying a permanent home, having kids, and living out the whole stay at home mom and working dad scenario seemed fitting. For millennials, generation Z; we want to travel more, pursue entrepreneurship, create our own brands and movements. We're not so focused on settling in, being structured, and grounded. We're catching flights; our imaginations are high in the sky. We're drifting away from the idea of school, college, job, and retire being the step by step game plan for life. We're moving passed being limited to certain religions, jobs, homes, and people for the rest of our lives. We're craving freedom. We're more fluid, in flow, and down for whatever. Were finally beginning to accept the fact that love is love no matter the gender or color. We're changing our diets, slowly but surely. We're wearing our natural hair. We're expressing our emotions. We're finally speaking on generational wounds and healing. We're dissolving and coagulating. The frequency of earth is rising and so are we. Flow with it instead of clinging onto the old paradigm patterns which no onger serve the evolution of the collective and the planet as a whole. This is a new age. When we surrender to the cycle we'll become one with the universe that is already us; **unconditional love.**

Chapter 16
Unconditional Love

Everything is Love

Everything we face, light or dark, low or high, is an expression of the universe teaching us how to love more unconditionally.

"If you want to know the secrets of the universe think in terms of energy, frequency, and vibration."
- **Nikola Tesla | Electrical Engineer, Inventor**

This is a quote I mentioned at the beginning of the book that probably is a whole lot easier to understand now. Everything is energy. To create a life of love within for one never without, ultimately it all comes down to authenticity, connection, spirituality, acceptance, peace, flow, and all other forms of unconditional love. Just be love and watch life shift in your favor.

This journey has brought me such a deep knowing of my true self. I have made such a profound transition and completed a major death and rebirth cycle. Within the whirlwind of the cycle I managed to simultaneously unlock the past me, before I started creating an identity out of survival, and the future me, a new identity built on love. Tyler brought me to and through this journey, and while here, I met Nala.....

To be continued.

Now that I've exchanged my understanding of everything I've learned so far in this phase of life, I guess this is where I leave you for now. Starting here, you will take whatever you desire from what I've shared and create the life your soul truly desires. Enjoy the journey. Here's a letter for your expedition, tear it out or leave it in but hold on to it in a way you always be able to come back to it when needed.

To you,
You is one bad ass, magical, divine, high vibrating, unstoppable, warrior. The universe responds to you; so be confident in all you do. Wholeheartedly believe you are magic. You are a spirit. You are fire, earth, water, and air. You are a flower and a tree of life. You are unconditional love. Your powerful line of ancestors, your angels, and the entire universe is rooting for you. Live up to the magnitude you can experience in this incredible life. Have fun, go on adventures, and always let your inner child live. You were born to live life out loud, so show the world what your made of.

Love, Nala

Acknowledgements

The way this entire book fell together is so universal; every chapter was perfectly placed how they should be. It's like it was already planned ahead of time for me to live my exact life, place my puzzle pieces together, experience a complete death of old self, and in the process of rebuilding myself create a beautiful piece of art to share with the world. Spirit, thank you for making my purpose, my life, my character, my experiences, and everything about me exactly the way it is. You're a real freaking artist in every form you come; life is your masterpiece.

As selfish as it may sound, I'd like to thank myself. I want to thank me for listening to my spirit, facing my biggest fears, and dedicating my life to love. Though I shared many of my trials I faced in this process; no one will ever understand the strength it took. Only another writer can empathize the strength it takes to pour out everything going on inside onto pages for others to read. Every day I fought with everything inside me to choose love over fear. Even when I wanted to give up on everything just to feel safe and comfortable, I kept going. I have to give huge props to myself. Good job Ty.

To my soul sister, my friend of many lifetimes, and mirror; Natasha. I want to thank you for sticking by my side through this entire process. Thank you for being a part of my life from a child to our adult years. You have such a huge impact on this creation you may not even understand. You mirrored wounds I needed to heal that I shared in this book. Your beautiful spirit and words of affirmation helped guide me. You told me with everything in you, you felt I should keep writing, so I did. At the time I started writing I had no idea what these writings would be. They started off as pages in my journals; you encouraged me to pour my heart out into these journals, to be vulnerable and authentic. Those journals then turned into blog post; those blog post didn't receive many views yet you still encouraged me to keep writing. Then those blog post turned into chapters.

When you told me to write, I had no idea all my lessons and all my heart aches would lead here to writing this book about my life to inspire many lives. Thank you twin; you forever my homie. This is only the beginning.

My dear beautiful mirror Aeryan; fashionista and kind heart. Thank you for your words; the words that inspired me to turned those blog post into chapters. You told me, "the way I explain things makes it easy for others to understand". This one sentence gave me the push I need to be put my fear and procrastination aside.

To my brothers, gang gang you already know wassup. Our bond is solid; It's all unconditional love no matter how far we are apart. Thank you for our memories through several phases of life. Thank you for your loyalty and protection. Lil sis loves you more than you know.

To all souls I have come across in my journey throughout life, whether we are still connected, indifferent, or only served a season in each other's lives; thank you. You taught me lessons that molded me into who I am today. I wish you ALL peace, love, and happiness as you continue your journey.

Pac, through your poetic insight and raw storytelling in your music you inspire me to show up and show out. To never let nobody make me be quite, to Speak my truth, to let my voice be heard loud and clear. To not give a fuck in the most beautiful way. To have unconditional love and not just for my mama. You inspired me to transform minds, to keep it real, and heal. In this life I lead, I ain't worried bout a damn thing, with this unconditional love I have flowing in me.

Nipsey, you left this world on the same day I celebrate entering it. Though it hurt to see one of my favorite artist transition on my day of birth you empowered me with the print you left in this world. Lighting a fire within me, reminding me what passion truly is; you gotta be willing to die behind your purpose. Your dreams manifest when you keep pushing, failing, and getting back up. You remind me that this shit is not a race, it's takes hard work, dedication, and patience. Your art, your mind, your spirit will forever inspire. I will run this marathon with love in my heart.

Jhené, got damn you such a beautiful soul. Your vulnerability, emotional depth, creativity, and dreamy Pisces energy reminds me to feel. To let life knock me down, to meet my darkness and become friends with it, only to release it and create from the whole process.

Cole, Hov, Lauryn, Miguel and every artist who has inspired me through your music. You remind me to express myself, creatively, always. Thank you.

Harriet, you show me the real definition of courage. I've read your story and studied the footsteps you left behind. You show what following your intuition through this journey of life without letting fear hinder your purpose looks like. You let it motivate you; bringing you closer to your own strength and reminding you your light was always stronger. I see a manifestation of true leadership and bravery. This you reflect in me, encouraging me to keep going, not only to free myself, but to free my people.

Thank you Jen Sincero, author of *You Are a Badass* [17]. You helped me unmask my inner badass. You inspired me to change the direction of my life and live it my way.

Shout out to *Spirit Science* on YouTube [18]. The information both scientific and spiritual you expose to the world to is so impactful. You challenged me to understand my world on a much deeper perspective. Thank you for your hard work to raise the consciousness of life on earth. You have invited openness to many perspectives.

To the creative director of *A Wrinkle in Time* [4], you're a genius. That's all I have to say.

Thank you to the director of *Life Itself* [7]; this movie has made the biggest impact on my story more than any movie I've ever watched. The message brought me to tears for hours on end as I felt a message from my spirit. In part of the movie the dying mother goes on to tell her young son, how there are many ups and downs in life. But, when we learn to heal, stand up, and move forward with life we will always find love. She explains how our lives and our stories are a continuation of our ancestors and will continue with our children after we are gone. The movie then flashes to the future; the grandchild of this same dying mother is now an adult. She has written a book about her story and how she got there. In her book release speech, she repeats the same words her grandmother said right before she died. She explains how we are a continuation of our grandmothers, grandfathers, mothers, and fathers. When we push through all life's tragedies and just keep going, we will always find love. The Young son of the mother grew up and listened to his mother's spirit; he kept going further. He then told his wife and daughter the words his mother whispered to him; he kept going and he found love for generations. The moment I heard this message was the moment I knew without a single doubt that I was meant to write this book. My entire life, and even those before mine have been leading to the culmination of this masterpiece.

Most of all I want to thank my family: to mama and daddy, my biggest supporters. Thank you for my childhood; for instilling the idea I could do absolutely anything I put my mind to. You taught me to be a dreamer, thinking, and doer. Your influence as a kind hearted nurturer and a selfless hard worker have taught me to live life with dedication and heart; as an entrepreneur and healer. Thank you for supporting me through every move I make; even when you don't understand. My number one supporters; I wouldn't trade you for the world. I love you. I want to give thanks to my grandparents, my big sister and big brother, my aunties and uncles, my cousins, my niece and nephews, and as far back as blood can go; thank you. Thank you for your role in my life, for loving me, protecting me, and creating the family I've been blessed with. To all my ancestors before me, thank you for your search for love and your strength to keep pushing and fighting through all life tragedies. It has brought me to this exact place in my life where I have found love in me and all around me. Because you decided to get back up from your knees in times you thought things couldn't get any lower, I am here writing this story; our story. This pain and darkness we have faced is now transmuting into light for the rest of humanity to come; our love story is infinite. My beautiful family and my ancestors; alive and gone you fought for love and I will make damn sure **love starts here**.

Notes

1. "Bruce Tainio and Tainio Technology Wave Quantum." *Wave Quantum* , 3 Feb. 2021, wavequantumblog.uk/2021/02/03/bruce-tainio/.
2. Buis , Alan. "Milankovitch (Orbital) Cycles and Their Role in Earth's Climate." *NASA Global Climate Change* , 27 Feb. 2020, climate.nasa.gov/news/2948/milankovitch-orbital-cycles-and-their-role-in-earths-climate/.
3. Chapman, Gary D. *The Five Love Languages: How to Express Heartfelt Commitment to Your Mate*. Northfield Pub., 2004.
4. DeVerney , Ava, director. *A Wrinkle in Time* . *Netflix* , Walt Disney Studios Motion Picture , 2018.
5. "Dr. Sebi's Nutritional Guide - ." *Dr. Sebi's Cell Food,* drsebiscellfood.com/pages/nutritional-guide.
6. Editorial Staff. "How Much Sodium Should I Eat per Day?" *American Heart Association* , 1 Nov. 2021, www.heart.org/en/healthy-living/healthy-eating/eat-smart/sodium/how-much-sodium-should-i-eat-per-day.
7. Folgelman, Dan, director. *Life Itself. Amazon Prime* , Amazon Studios , 2018.
8. "The Human Eye Can Only See between 430-770 Thz." *The Minds Journal*, 2 Feb. 2023, themindsjournal.com/quotes/the-human-eye-can-only-see-between-430-770-thz/.
9. Lipton, Bruce H. *The Biology of Belief: Unleashing the Power of Consciousness, Matter & Miracles*. Hay House, 2016.
10. Lynch, William. *The Willie Lynch Letter ; the Making of a Slave*. Lushena Books, 1999.
11. Mercola . "If You Wear Make-Up, Your Body Could Be Absorbing Up to 5 Lbs of Chemicals Per Year." *Organic Consumers Association* , 22 June 2007, organicconsumers.org/article_6013/#.

12. Ocean, Frank. "Pyramids ." *Channel Orange*, Def Jam.
13. *The Post Traumatic Slave Diet* , YouTube , 2 Mar. 2016, www.youtube.com/watch?v=I-GQYK-UrRQ.
14. "Protecting Consumers as the Buyers and Users of Cosmetic Products in the Light of European Parliament and Council Regulation (EC) No 1223/2009 on Cosmetic Products." *Official Journal of the European Union*, no. 8(968), 2017, doi:10.15678/znuek.2017.0968.0803.
15. Semega, Jessica, Melissa Kollar, Emily A. Shrider, and John F. Creamer U.S. Census Bureau, Current Population Reports, P60-270 (RV), Income and Poverty in the United States: 2019, U.S. Government Publishing Office, Washington, DC, 2020.
16. Shakur, Tupac. "Changes." *Greatest Hits*, Death Row Records/Interscope Records.
17. Sincero, Jen. *You Are a Badass*. Running Press, 2017.
18. "Spirit Science ." *YouTube*, YouTube, www.youtube.com/.
19. Tesla, Nikola. *My Inventions: The Autobiography of Nikola Tesla*. 2014.
20. Zimmer , Carl. "How Many Cells Are In Your Body?" *National Geographic* , 23 Oct. 2013, www.nationalgeographic.com/science/article/how-many-cells-are-in-your-body.

A Natural Lifestyle Movement

Natural; our truest and most raw form. Whether it be on a physical level; our natural hair, body, and skin. On a mental level; our true thoughts and free flowing imagination. On an emotional level; our emotions naturally running through us, even the hard ones. Or, on a spiritual level; our passions, natural born gifts, and the natural depth of our souls. Either way, whether we embrace one or all of one of things, they begin to reveal a certain light from within.

A natural lifestyle is about healing, loving, nourishing, and expressing our true self by gaining inspiration and aligning with the rawness of nature. It's not about being perfect, ultimately it's a movement toward self-improvement, health, authenticity, and self-love. Being any part of our most natural form is what opens up our aura and allows our inner light to GLOW.

JOIN THE MOVEMENT and use the tag

#Naturalisthewaytoglow

The All Natural is your One Stop Holistic Health Shop; providing ALL your needs for healing for being and healing all of you; mind, body, emotion, and spirit.

Here at The All Natural, we innerstand and give gratitude for the power of nature and its ability to align us with our most healthy, whole, and authentic self.

Website: Theallnatural.co

Facebook: The All Natural

Instagram: Theallnaturalco

Twitter: @ __OfficialTAN

LinkedIN: The All Natural

A safe and sacred space where WE sip our tea and talk the REAL tea; how to heal thyself.

Every other Tuesday CEO & Founder of The All Natural and author of Love Starts Here, Nala Asa Shakur host her series #TTALK where she discusses healing thyself and finding our path to love, truth, wholeness, authenticity! Nala refers to her book and uses various spiritual tools to give and receive an overall healing experience. All while she and her listeners enjoy a nice cup of tea!

Instagram: Tatlkpodcast

TikTok: Ttalkpodcast

Youtube: Ttalkpodcast